A Visual History of
Modern Britain

Edited by
Professor Jack Simmons

Transport

Jack Simmons

Vista Books

©
Jack Simmons
1962

First published by
VISTA BOOKS
Longacre Press Ltd, 161–166 Fleet St, London,
EC4
Printed in Great Britain by
The Anchor Press Ltd, Tiptree, Essex

Contents

List of Illustrations

The author and the publishers are grateful to all those who have co-operated in searching for and supplying pictures and to those who have given permission for them to be reproduced. Large collections frequently drawn upon are indicated by the following abbreviations: B.M. (British Museum), B.T.C.H.R. (British Transport Commission: Historical Relics Dept), N.B.R. (National Buildings Record), R.T.H.P.L. (Radio Times Hulton Picture Library), S.M. (Science Museum, South Kensington), V. & A. (Victoria and Albert Museum). Nos. 26 and 222 are Crown Copyright, reproduced by permission of The Controller of H.M. Stationery Office.

LIST OF ILLUSTRATIONS

Editor's Introduction

The purpose of this *Visual History* is to provide, largely by means of pictures, an account of the social history of modern Britain. The attempt is no novelty in itself; but some of the principles on which it is based are new. They must be explained if the scope, and the limitations, of the series are to be understood.

The use of a text based both on pictures and on words requires, I hope, no justification. For the document, the picture, and the object in a museum are all important alike in helping us to understand the life of the past, and they need to be treated together if they are to reveal their full significance.

It is an essential part of the plan of the *Visual History* that the illustrations should be authentic, not conjectural. They comprise therefore either pictures contemporary with the scenes and events they portray or photographs of contemporary objects. Reconstructions, however ingenious or convincing, are excluded. In most fields, contemporary pictures begin to become available from the fifteenth century onwards. The main weight of this work therefore falls on the past 500 years, though one or two subjects can usefully be treated from a somewhat earlier date.

It is a corollary of this principle that the pictures chosen should be from England, Wales, or Scotland. In many previous pictorial histories—including one of the best of them, *The Life and Work of the People of England*, by Dorothy Hartley and Margaret Elliot—Continental pictures were freely admitted, often without any indication that they came from abroad. On occasion the use of foreign examples may be absolutely necessary; but such cases will be rare, and each will be specifically noted in the caption attached to the picture.

In selecting the pictures, a special effort has been made to exploit the great collections of material that are assembled in the museums, galleries, and libraries of Britain outside London. Inevitably, such great London collections as those of the British Museum and the National Buildings Record must be heavily drawn upon; but the vast body of pictures and museum objects to be seen today in the English provinces, in Wales, and in

Scotland has been very little studied by historians. I hope that this series of books may do something to reveal the astonishing wealth of material that has been accumulated, over the past century and more, in these places; especially since now, with modern techniques of display, much of it is so delightfully presented.

The plan of the *Visual History* is not based, like most of its predecessors, on a division by period. Instead, it is divided by subject. Though each volume is self-contained, it will gain from being read in conjunction with the rest. Some important subjects will inevitably cut across the division adopted for the series as a whole. Thus the evolution of local government will be treated both in the volume on *The Town* and in that on *Government*; the history of trade will be discussed, from different aspects, in *The Town*, in *Transport*, and in *Industry*. Such cross-references will, I hope, be valuable in themselves, helping to emphasise the inter-dependence of all parts of the whole great theme: the evolution of modern Britain.

J.S.

Prologue

TRANSPORT IS A SERVICE that every one now takes for granted. Like television and radio, like the system of drainage in towns, like the police force, we assume it is there; to be made use of as it suits our own convenience, part of the accepted conditions of life today. Yet any one who is concerned with the past, with the stages and the means by which Britain came to be what she is now, will realise that none of these things can be presupposed. In 1945 the ordinary citizen had no television; in 1920 he never heard a radio programme; a century ago few towns had main drainage; the police force, as we know it, dates only from 1829. There has been transport in this island, in some recognisable form, for 3,000 years and more. But it has been subject to strict limitations, according to the methods employed. Within those limitations, transport has done much to shape the economic, the social, and the political development of Britain.

Changes in transport, for example, have helped to determine the rise and fall of towns. Darlington, Holyhead, and Grimsby grew rich in consequence of them. Shaftesbury and Boroughbridge decayed. Abingdon prospered as a result of one such change in the fifteenth century ⟨14⟩* and fell back because of another in the nineteenth. Stourport ⟨59–61⟩ and Goole owe their origin to the canals, Crewe and Eastleigh to the railways. The development of coal production, on which so much of the economic power of Britain has rested, depended at all times on the provision of adequate transport, by water and by land. The same thing is true, to an even greater degree, of some other industries, which could not develop at all without fundamental changes in transport: the potteries of Staffordshire, for example, the cultivation of early flowers and vegetables in Cornwall and the Channel Islands. Transport, too, has helped to mould the conditions of political life: whether in the English Civil War, in the Highlands of Scotland after the Jacobite Rebellions ⟨53⟩, or in the quiet Parliamentary government of the twentieth century ⟨218⟩.

* The numbers in diamond brackets, e.g. ⟨14⟩, refer to the illustrations on page 71 onwards. The superior figures in the text refer to the Notes on pages 209–12.

1

This book is concerned with inland transport in all its branches, both separately and in relation to one another. It also considers coastal shipping, which for most economic purposes must be regarded as an integral part of the internal transport system. It has been well said that, where transport is concerned, 'the sea becomes merely a river round England, a river with peculiar dangers, peculiar conditions, and peculiar advantages'.[1] Those words were applied to the Britain of the seventeenth century. They apply to her also in the different conditions of the twentieth.

In any history of transport a prominent place must be taken by technical changes. It is so here: such changes provide the titles of three of the five chapters that follow. Yet they must not be over-emphasised. For all the romantic legends, like that of Watt and the boiling kettle, the truth is that technical improvements arise rarely from abstract speculation, but most usually from new economic and social needs, which direct the thinking of engineers, as of other people, to the ways of meeting them. The railway owes much indeed to George Stephenson, but his triumphs and the thought that lay behind them were governed by the problems that had to be solved, within certain defined limits, at a particular time. It is only when those problems are grasped that the working of the inventor's mind and the true nature of his creative imagination are rightly understood. In this study we shall be concerned primarily with the successive demands that a changing society made on its transport system; and that will be our standpoint for looking at the life and work of the engineers, and at the machines they produced.

Our knowledge of the development of transport derives not only from written sources. We learn much about it from maps, from pictorial records of all kinds, and from the relics of the past that remain. These are very numerous: old buildings and equipment still in use, or surviving disused on the spot and in museums; relics elsewhere of many different kinds, in unlikely places such as churches ⟨101⟩, private houses, and pubs. It is this kind of evidence that makes up the second part of the book.

The Middle Ages

THERE WERE THREE main elements in the transport system of the Middle Ages: coastal shipping, river navigation, and roads.

Coastal shipping furnished the most suitable means of carrying bulky freight originating near the sea. Coal was transported in this way from the Tyne to London from the closing years of the twelfth century. The first coal shipped may have come from Tynemouth, where it could be taken from workings on the shore; but very soon the chief source came to be the much larger fields of Gateshead and Whickham, south of the Tyne, both of which belonged to the bishop of Durham. For these fields the most convenient port of shipment was Newcastle, already a substantial town, protected by Henry II's great stone keep and engaged in trade with Flanders and France. The townsmen quickly tried to secure for themselves the control of this valuable new traffic and embarked on a long and tough struggle to this end with the bishops and the priors of Tynemouth. They triumphed only with the Reformation.

Most of the ships that carried this coal in the Middle Ages were owned by foreigners. They sailed up from the Continent or from southern England with cargoes of grain, which they exchanged for cloth, fish, and grindstones (the chief marketable products of north-eastern England); and at first they regarded coal as valuable chiefly for ballast. In the course of the thirteenth century coal became a profitable form of merchandise in its own right, though before the Tudor period the annual export from the Tyne seldom exceeded 15,000 tons.

In Scotland a similar export of coal grew up from the field of Tranent in East Lothian. Edinburgh took much of it; but it is worth noting that though the distance from Tranent was only ten miles, across easy country, the coal was taken down to the coast, shipped to Leith, and then hauled up the steep slope to the town. Tranent coal was also consigned in some quantity to Perth and Dundee, and it found its way as far north as Aberdeen, Inverness, Orkney, and Shetland.[2]

Another heavy commodity, in much greater demand during the Middle Ages, was building stone. This, too, was transported largely by sea. That Caen stone became fashionable in England after the Conquest is to be explained not only by the conservative preference of the Normans for stone of their own country, but by the ease with which it could be shipped up the Channel. Similarly, Purbeck marble could not possibly have enjoyed its great vogue in the thirteenth century if the quarries from which it was drawn had not been close to the sea, which provided a ready means of transport: to London, for example, to the Wash for Ely, to the Humber for Lincoln and York.

The transport of building stone illustrates very well the interlocking facilities provided by the sea and the rivers. Occasionally almost the entire haul could be made by sea. When Purbeck marble and stone from the quarries at Beer in East Devon were used in the reconstruction of Exeter cathedral in the thirteenth and fourteenth centuries, they were shipped to Topsham and thence carted (by the Chapter's own tenants, as part of their

3

customary service) for the remaining half-dozen miles. Nearly all the grea quarries of medieval Britain lay on the coast or near navigable water: Dryburgh on the Tweed, for example, Frosterley on the Wear, Tadcaster on the Wharfe, the 'Kentish rag' quarries near Maidstone on the Medway. The great quarries that straddle Stamford—Ketton and Barnack—were ideally placed for the distribution of their stone; for the Welland, by which they lay, joined up with the whole system of Fenland rivers and so enabled it to be floated up into Northamptonshire, Cambridgeshire and East Anglia or out through the Wash into the North Sea. Many of the great monasteries of eastern England—Peterborough, Ramsey, Crowland, Bury St. Edmunds —rented quarries at Barnack. Sawtry Abbey in Huntingdonshire had a quarry there too, and in the late twelfth century cut a canal, half a dozen miles long, from Sawtry to Whittlesea Mere expressly for the purpose of transporting the stone needed for its building. In 1301 Norwich cathedral was buying stone both from Barnack and from Caen, to be brought up the Yare from the sea.[3]

It would be wrong to suppose, however, that the navigation of rivers in medieval England was a simple matter. Even the greatest of them were full of obstructions, and dangerous in time of flood. The Severn was navigable for large vessels as high as Bewdley and for smaller craft up to Shrewsbury; the great tides of the Bristol Channel scoured the river's mouth and prevented it from silting up like the Dee and the Kentish Stour. It was distinguished among the larger English rivers by being, in fact as well as in theory, a 'free river'—free, that is, to any one to travel or convey his goods along its whole length without paying toll. Other rivers were recognised as free only within their tidal limits: thus the Humber was free, but the city of York had jurisdiction over the Ouse. On the Severn the only tolls that might be taken were those specifically allowed to certain towns on its banks for the privilege of transacting business there. Gloucester, for example, was authorised in 1335 to exact 4d. from each ship arriving with goods for sale; the money so raised to be spent on the town's paving.

Both for physical and for economic reasons the Severn was the greatest waterway in medieval Britain. Yet the navigation along it was continually obstructed, above all by piracy and by the erection of mills and weirs. 'Piracy' is not too strong a term to apply to the depredations of the men of the Forest of Dean (an unruly people at all times) and of Bewdley, a town that rose much in importance in the early fifteenth century and wished to assert itself against its older and greater rivals, Worcester and Gloucester. Such lawlessness flourished under the weak government of Henry VI; but his successors were better able to police the country, and they put it down. The building of weirs and mills was harder to stop, for it reflected a genuine and continuing economic conflict between three groups:

4

those who wished to use the water of the rivers for fishing, for power, and for transport. Early in the thirteenth century, Chapter 33 of Magna Carta condemned the introduction of fish-kiddles (dams with a centre opening, across which a net could be stretched) as nuisances obstructing navigation, which ought to be free to all the King's subjects, and the condemnation was repeated again and again in Acts of Parliament. But the repetition shows that the attempt to prohibit the practice had been ineffective. In the same way the miller would build a cut at the side of the river to divert water for turning his wheel: water that was precious, at all times except those of flood, for keeping river craft afloat. Moreover, to secure a proper head of water in the cut it was usual for a weir to be built alongside, to hold the river back. If the river was navigable, the centre of the weir would be made to open for the passage of boats. This was what was called a flash-lock or (in eastern England) a staunch ⟨198⟩.

Such arrangements led to endless dispute. The Government made an attempt to settle the question in 1351, in favour of transport interests, by ordering the removal of all obstructions that had been erected in rivers since 1307. Once more the ineffectiveness of the measure is shown by the necessity for re-enacting it twenty years later, with the enormous fine of 100 marks to be incurred by offenders in future. It may be that some progress was then made, since the legislation of succeeding years was directed against older obstructions; but the problem was never solved, and it was particularly acute on the Thames.

Though some efforts were thus made to improve the navigation of the greater rivers, we know of only one attempt to develop a major artificial waterway in this country during the Middle Ages, though minor cuts were sometimes made, usually for military purposes ⟨7⟩. The Romans had built up a considerable canal system in Lincolnshire and the Fenland, which joined the Cam and the Wash to the Trent, by way of Peterborough and Lincoln. Much of this system was allowed to fall into disuse—some parts of it even within the Roman period. In 1121, however, Henry I re-opened the Foss Dyke from Lincoln to Torksey, a very important cut that joined the Witham to the Trent.*

When the navigation of the greater rivers was impeded by so many obstacles, it was harder still to pass traffic along the smaller ones. Too sweeping an assumption has often been made that all heavy traffic in the Middle Ages went by water. In fact, land transport was often preferred, at least to a point at which the goods could be shipped on to an easily navigable river. Merton College bought large quantities of stone from the great

* It must be said that the Roman origin of the Lincolnshire canals has never been conclusively proved, though there is strong archaeological evidence to support it. The Car Dyke in Cambridgeshire is, however, certainly Roman.

5

Taynton quarries, west of Burford, all through the fourteenth century. It was not, as we might suppose, put into boats on the Windrush, a fair-sized river only a mile below, and so taken down to Oxford. Instead, it was hauled in carts to Eynsham, over a dozen miles away, and there loaded on to the Thames.[4]

This opens up an important problem, which has given rise to much controversy and still needs further investigation. What was the state of land transport during the Middle Ages, and how much use was made of it?

The discussion of this question has been dominated, and often bedevilled, by a misplaced emphasis on the roads of Roman Britain ⟨1⟩. It is perfectly true that the Romans built up a system of trunk roads that was allowed to decay after their departure and was not equalled again for some 1,300 years, until the early nineteenth century. Both in laying out roads and in draining and surfacing them, they were infinitely superior to their Saxon and medieval successors. Nevertheless, it must be remembered that the purposes served by the Roman and the medieval roads were in some respects different. The Roman system in Britain was devised in the first place with a view to military needs. It provided for the rapid transit of passengers, in wheeled vehicles as well as on horseback, throughout the whole of the settled part of the province. A very substantial network of by-roads was also developed, to serve economic purposes such as the transport of iron from the Weald of Kent and Sussex.[5]

In the political disturbances that succeeded the Roman rule, many of the purposes their roads had served lost their importance. Britain was fragmented into separate kingdoms; and by the time almost the whole of what we now call England was reunited under one government in the ninth century most of the Roman trunk roads had fallen into disuse as thoroughfares, though many sections of them continued to serve either as local highways or as clear and well-marked boundaries. Still, four main roads were regarded as 'the King's highways' in a special class: Watling Street, the Foss Way, the Icknield Way, and Ermine Street. They formed the main framework of the country's internal communications, linking Dover and London with Chester and the Humber, with cross-roads running eastwards to the Wash and south-westwards to Devonshire.

Little was done to keep these roads, or any others, in good repair—nothing that would have stood a Roman engineer's scrutiny. But then they were not intended, as the Roman roads had been, for fast wheeled traffic. They were used chiefly by passengers on horseback and by goods carried slowly on packhorses or in carts, hauled as a rule by oxen. Moreover, their main purpose was not to provide rapid transit for long distances. They were used much more intensively to link neighbouring towns and villages with one another, and especially to afford access to weekly markets

6

and occasional fairs. Markets were far more numerous in the Middle Ages than they are today. Hundreds were established, up and down the country, that have long since fallen into disuse; markets in what are now small villages or hamlets, or in settlements whose very names have disappeared. There were some eighty in Devon in the fourteenth century.[6] Think how many places bear the name 'Market' or 'Chipping' (its Old English equivalent) that are now to be reckoned villages: Market Lavington (Wilts.), Market Overton (Rutland), Chipping Warden (Northants.), Chipping in the remotest part of Lancashire under Longridge Fell. All these places, and hundreds more, once saw their crowds coming on foot or riding or leading packhorses and carts: by some sort of road, good or bad.

In one respect a great deal was certainly done to improve road communications in the Middle Ages: by the building of bridges. The earlier bridges were usually built of timber. Gradually, however, they came to be replaced by more durable structures in stone. At Bideford, indeed, the thirteenth-century wooden bridge was used as scaffolding for the larger work in stone that succeeded it in about 1460: the bridge that, with some later alterations, stands now ⟨13⟩. One of the oldest major bridges to remain virtually unaltered to this day is that at Huntingdon, rebuilt in its present form about 1300 ⟨10⟩. Many of these bridges carried houses, like Old London Bridge ⟨27⟩, which was reconstructed in stone over a period of thirty years, beginning in 1176, and—a surviving example—the High Bridge at Lincoln ⟨28⟩. Chapels were built on them, like those still to be seen at Rotherham and Wakefield; many were fortified, such as those at Monmouth ⟨11⟩ and Newcastle ⟨8⟩.

Much money was spent on these works, partly from private benefaction, encouraged by the Church, partly from taxation authorised by the State. The skill of the engineers responsible for them is demonstrated by their continued survival to the present day in substantial numbers. In surveys made about thirty years ago some 150 bridges wholly or partly of medieval date were recorded in England and Wales.[7]

The medieval road system comprised something more than the sum of an infinite number of small highways leading to local markets. Besides the four 'King's highways' there were others that could be described as trunk roads, such as that which ran from Bristol by way of Gloucester and the Severn Valley to Chester. In the later Middle Ages a series of main highways can be said to emerge, radiating from London. Though they run in part along a Roman alignment, none of them corresponds closely to a Roman road. They are in fact to be regarded as new roads, though they were not deliberately constructed as such. (The making of a wholly new road is recorded very rarely in medieval England, and then only for military purposes, as when Henry I built a road across Wenlock Edge in 1102.) They

B

were developed gradually, almost unconsciously, to meet a new political need: for communication between London and the centres of government in the provinces. Under the Angevin and Plantagenet kings, England was the most highly centralised monarchy in Europe; and as London became more and more clearly the fixed seat of government and the economic capital of the country, so the use of the roads leading to and from it increased. Water transport was always vital to London, for imports by sea and for the traffic on the Thames. But the Thames was its sole river. The Chilterns interposed a barrier between London and the rest of the country's waterways. The Midlands and the North could be reached with speed only by road.

We are fortunate in having a remarkable map of the English road system dating from the fourteenth century. It is called the Gough Map, not from its compiler but from the antiquary Richard Gough who bequeathed it in 1809 to the Bodleian Library, where it remains. The work shows every sign of minute care—the author, for example, refusing to include any road on which he could not give the distance in miles from point to point, even though he indicated the places that he knew to lie along its route. The map comprehends the whole of Great Britain, but the same scrupulousness prevented the compiler from pretending to knowledge that he did not really possess of Wales and Scotland. The only Welsh roads he indicates are one running along the north coast from Chester to Caernarvon, one from Caernarvon to Criccieth and along the coast to Cardigan, and a third from Hereford to Brecon and thence to an indeterminate point further west. He marks no Scottish roads at all, though he indicates the rivers and chief towns of southern and eastern Scotland with a fair degree of accuracy.

One thing that emerges very clearly from the Gough Map is the existence of a road system based on London: a road system that owes something to its Roman ancestry yet has taken on a pattern entirely its own, suited to the political and economic needs of Plantagenet England.[8]

The fifteenth century is frequently represented as a vicious and dreary age in British history, characterised by the futile splendours of the later part of the Hundred Years' War, the ferocious and ignoble Wars of the Roses, the dismal cycles of political murder in Scotland. In the history of transport, however, it is very clearly an age of improvement.

Successive governments now began to display a new and constructive interest in shipping. Under Henry V this was primarily a response to the military needs of the French war. It led the king to develop a royal navy, on a scale much more formidable than that of any earlier English fleet, including several ships bigger than any previously built in this country; and this development, in turn, made it possible for his Government, for a short time at least, to police the Channel and give full protection to English

8

merchant shipping against the pirates—English, Breton, and French—
who had constantly endangered its security. With the death of Henry V,
this effort collapsed. The reign of his weak successor Henry VI is filled
with demands for the better 'keeping of the seas', of which the political
poem called *The Libel of English Policy* (1436) is the best known. Though
they were met inadequately, they reflect the growing importance of
English mercantile and shipping interests, which were strong enough to
force the Yorkist and Tudor governments to pay attention to their
grievances and to give them what help lay in their power.

Though little is known in detail of medieval Scottish shipping, it was
undoubtedly fostered by the Government in the fifteenth century, especially under James IV. Acts of Parliament of 1493 and 1503 enjoined shipbuilding; and the King showed off in the accepted manner of the time by
commissioning a warship of exceptionally large size, the *Great Michael*,
launched apparently in 1511 and sold three years later, after the death of
James IV at Flodden, to the French Government, which in the end allowed
her to rot away at Brest. The Scottish Treasurer's accounts of the time
provide interesting information about the sources from which the materials
for the *Great Michael* and her contemporaries were derived: timber from
Norway, brasswork from Denmark, rigging from the Netherlands and
France. Nothing from England except Cornish tin, for the gunsmiths; and
that was not bought direct, but in Antwerp.[9]

The English were now beginning to free themselves from their past
dependence on foreign shipping. It is true that the trade with the Mediterranean, on which Southampton flourished in the fifteenth century, was in
the hands of Italians and conveyed in large ships from Genoa and Venice.
The Hanseatic League, moreover, continued to control most of the valuable
trade between England and the Baltic. Yet English merchants and seamen
of the east-coast ports and Bristol were becoming increasingly involved in
the Iceland trade, and towards the close of the century English ships were
beginning to feel their way out westwards into the ocean. It has been truly
said of the men of Bristol that 'though the volume of their trade was as
yet comparatively small, their knowledge of the seas was now wider than
that of either of the traditional sea-powers of Europe, who so stubbornly
resisted their intrusion':[10] for they knew both the Italians' Mediterranean
and the Hansa men's northern waters besides a great tract of the Atlantic
that was at present entirely their own. It is not surprising that the first
of the great English 'shipping magnates'—men who amassed very large
fortunes primarily through the owning of ships—was a Bristolian of these
years, William Canynges (see also *The Town*, p. 17 and plate 30).

In the early part of the fifteenth century a revolution took place in the
design of ships in northern Europe. It was 'the time when the development

9

of the sailing ship went on at a faster pace than at any other period in history';[11] when the full-rigged ship, with three or more masts, established itself as the standard type, in all essentials the same as that which lasted until sail was ousted by steam. Before 1400 the northern ships had only one mast; those of the Mediterranean had two. Now the two types influenced each other, to emerge fused as the full-rigged ship, with three masts: an adequate instrument for the great oceanic voyages of Columbus and Drake. At the same time, moreover, the northern shipwrights abandoned the practice of clinker-building (with the planks of the hull overlapping) in favour of carvel-building, in which the planks were laid edge to edge. This broke a long tradition. The ships of the north had been clinker-built at least since the third century A.D.; carvel-building, on the other hand, had been the accepted practice in the Mediterranean since the time of the Roman Empire, and probably for much longer still. These great changes were a direct consequence of the increased intercourse between northern and southern Europe, and owed much to the critically important influence of the ships and seamen of Bayonne.

We can follow these changes well in contemporary pictorial records—on seals and coins, in stained glass and bench-ends as well as in drawings. But it must be remembered that the craftsmen responsible had usually no knowledge of ships themselves. Unless they were closely directed by somebody who was skilled in nautical matters, the result might be a merely conventional representation, a travesty of what the ship really looked like. Moreover, one must always bear in mind the medium in which the artist was working. If he was designing a seal or a coin he would inevitably give the ship's hull, to an exaggerated degree, a semicircular line; on a bench-end everything would be distorted vertically. It will not do, therefore, to expect a detailed and faithful representation of something so technically complex as a ship. Yet, when these necessary allowances have been made, here is a valuable indication of the stages by which successive developments came about: the introduction of the stern rudder, for example ⟨3⟩, the appearance of the full-rigged ship.

These changes in the size of ships coincided with, and to some extent helped to bring about, changes in the economic geography of southern England. Physically, the English coast of the Channel falls into two divisions, of which the boundary line falls near Swanage.[12] To the west the coast has been, in historic times, relatively stable; eastwards, and especially east of the Solent, it is subject to constant erosion, its bays and lagoons solidify, its river-mouths silt up with drifting material in the sea. The Cinque Ports were killed from this cause, mainly during the fifteenth century. The great Italian ships, which had for some time past called at Southampton and Sandwich, abandoned Sandwich before the century was

10

out. By then Winchelsea was no longer to be reckoned a port at all, and in Henry VII's reign merchants were leaving the town. Its occupation was gone, it was fast sinking into the timeless trance in which we see it today: a medieval port high up on dry land (see *The Town*, plate 5). The bigger ships that were now coming into use could not negotiate harbours like these. They sought London, Southampton, and the western ports instead.

This was indeed a golden age for Southampton, as the main *entrepôt* of the valuable trade with North Italy. Recent research, too, has revealed a striking characteristic in the handling of this trade.[13] Though the town stands at the mouth of the Itchen and close to that of the Test, those are inconsiderable rivers, which boasted only two towns of any importance in the Middle Ages, Winchester and Romsey. If the great cargoes of spices and manufactured goods were to find adequate markets, it had to be by means of coastal shipping or by road. The greater part went by road; carriers' services were in operation to London, to Bristol, and even to places as far north as Manchester and Kendal. It is surprising to find that consignments for ports not far along the coast, such as Poole, might be sent by land. Clearly by the middle of the fifteenth century the distribution of goods could be easily and efficiently undertaken by road throughout southern England and the Midlands.

Some striking works of road improvement were undertaken at this time. One example may be mentioned, which is still in part to be seen ⟨14⟩. In the fourteenth century Abingdon had a considerable manufacture of cloth,

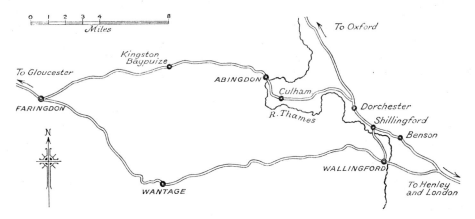

and its citizens engaged in an unsuccessful struggle with the abbots for the control of their government. Baulked here, some of them, earnest members of the Gild of the Holy Cross, turned their energies to a great public improvement: the replacing of the unsatisfactory ford across the Thames to the west of the town by a bridge, to be connected by a causeway to a second

11

bridge across another reach of the river at Culham. This work was begun in 1416 and apparently completed in 1437. Since the bridge and causeway were not only built but maintained by the wealthy gild, it was possible to keep them free of toll from the start.

The consequence of this new work soon became clear. It was to put Abingdon on to a main road from London to Gloucester, replacing that which spanned the Thames at Wallingford. The bridge at Wallingford was reported in 1429 to be ruinous and a cause of accidents to those who crossed it; nor was it fully repaired until the eighteenth century. Though the work at Abingdon did not ruin Wallingford, which was already in economic difficulties, it took that town permanently off the road to the west. The bridge was a good investment for Abingdon.[14]

The first Act of Parliament for improving the navigation of a single river was passed in 1424, in respect of the Lea. This measure also represents the earliest known example of a procedure that came to govern much of the subsequent development of transport in this country: the statutory establishment of a body of commissioners, with power to borrow money for the work and to levy tolls on those who made use of it for the repayment of the loan.

By this time it is becoming possible to make some firm statements about the speed of communication.[15] A sequence of recorded journeys between 1447 and 1497 shows that the regular time from Exeter to London (about 170 miles) on horseback was then three or four days. On special occasions, such as the carrying of important political news, higher speeds were possible. The murder of James I at Perth in 1437 was known in London, 440 miles south, exactly a week later. In 1497 the news of Perkin Warbeck's landing at the far extremity of Cornwall reached Henry VII at Woodstock (270 miles away) in three days. The arrival of Catherine of Aragon, as a young bride, at Plymouth in 1501 was reported in London two days later. On that occasion the news must have travelled at the rate of about 100 miles a day. This may be regarded as the greatest speed that could be looked for; it must have required organised relays of horses, and probably of messengers too. Such a system as that had been employed by Edward IV for the transmission of news during his Scottish campaign in 1482, perhaps in imitation of the more elaborate scheme established by Louis XI in France. It is not altogether far-fetched to see here the origins of the modern postal service.

During the fifteenth century, then, the transport system was expanded and improved. Like all peaceful activities, however, it required political stability, and that was an ideal seldom attained for long in Lancastrian and Yorkist England.

12

The Sixteenth and Seventeenth Centuries

SUCCESSIVE TUDOR GOVERNMENTS devoted much attention to the problems of transport, attempting general legislation over the whole field. Some of this was manifestly ineffective. Henry VII's Navigation Acts, for example, themselves a reassertion of principles laid down in the reign of Richard II, quickly became a dead letter through the want of power to enforce them. In the sixteenth century, however, several measures were passed that remained important for generations, even centuries, afterwards.

The first of them dates from the reign of Henry VIII. In 1514, moved by his active personal interest in ships and seamen, he issued a charter incorporating the Gild of Trinity House to foster 'the science or art of mariners', giving them power to make regulations 'for the relief, increase, and augmentation of the shipping of this our realm of England'. Though the charter did not create Trinity House (for the Fraternity was already in existence), it gave the Brethren a new authority and power; and when the gilds were dissolved in Edward VI's reign they were adroit enough to convert themselves into the Corporation they have remained ever since. Their work for the protection of shipping grew in scope, until they eventually came to control all lighthouses and lightships round the coast of England and Wales and to bear responsibility for pilots required by ships entering port. Trinity House is not an institution that figures much in the history textbooks: yet it has been an essential instrument in the growth of English maritime power ⟨108⟩.

In the same year the Thames watermen, whose services had been important in medieval London, were brought under the regulation of a statute. Its main purpose was to define the fares they should charge, ranging from four shillings for the hire of a barge to or from Gravesend to a penny for a short trip in London or Westminster. Forty years later, in 1555, the watermen came more closely under the Government's control, when eight of their number were appointed their 'overseers and rulers' and the outline of the later Watermen's Company emerged.

Another important measure of Henry VIII's reign was the Statute of Bridges of 1531. This was designed to settle the responsibility for the repair of all bridges, which had frequently been a matter of dispute. Those within corporate towns were to be a charge on the citizens; the rest were to be maintained by the counties—that is, under the authority of the Justices of the Peace in Quarter Sessions—unless it could be shown that by custom they had been repaired by the parishes, in which case the parishes were to continue liable. Where some private body had borne the responsibility, that was to remain unchanged: as with Rochester Bridge, which had been for some 200 years in the charge of Wardens, who have care of it to this day. The Act of 1531 did not remove all causes of dispute. Much argument was possible about the 'custom' that had obtained in the past. But it clearly empowered the Justices to see that bridges were kept in repair, and to levy the rates that were needed for this purpose. It remained the basis of the law concerning bridges in England until the nineteenth century.

Although it was the general principle throughout Britain that the repair and maintenance of bridges should be the responsibility of local authorities, there were a few that were recognised as being of national importance. As an example let us consider the bridge over the Tay at Perth, once described in a Scottish official document as 'the only band of the south and north parts of this country': without exaggeration, for the north-bound traveller from Edinburgh or Stirling could ride over the Tay only at this point. The repair of the bridge was normally the business of the Corporation of Perth. But it was a small and poor town, and when the bridge (which was built of timber and had to withstand the river's violent floods) fell into serious disrepair in the sixteenth century, the bailies found the task beyond their resources. Accordingly, in 1578, an Act was passed in the Scottish Parliament imposing a national levy of 10,000 marks to enable the work to be carried out. On the strength of this, it was decided to reconstruct the bridge in stone. The work went forward, however, at a snail's pace. The bailies leased a quarry at Pitheavlis, a mile to the west of the town, and found themselves engaged in a tiresome dispute with the owner, John Murray of Tibbermuir, which had to be referred to the Privy Council. By 1599 it appears that the work had been no more than begun. The Privy Council ordered Murray not to hinder the bailies further from taking the stone they needed; but things moved no faster. A committee was appointed in 1609 to investigate the spending of the money. The bridge was at last finished in time for a visit of the King to the town in 1617. But once again, four years later, the Tay proved too strong for it, and all but one arch was destroyed. The bridge then remained ruinous, and the stonework was pillaged by order of Cromwell for the building of the citadel on the South Inch in 1652. Travellers moving north had to be content with a service of ferry-boats, some thirty of which were in operation in the eighteenth century. A new stone bridge, strong enough to resist the violence of the river, was not provided until Smeaton built one in 1766–71 ⟨54⟩.[16]

Another attempt to fix an important administrative and financial responsibility was made in the Highways Act passed in the reign of Philip and Mary in 1555. In the Middle Ages the responsibility for maintaining roads had usually lain with the courts of the manors through which they passed; urban streets were a corporate charge on towns, sometimes assisted, as we have seen in the case of Gloucester, by a grant of the right to levy tolls for their repair. Funds were often available, too, for this purpose from private benefaction and from the town gilds, some of which—like the Gild of the Holy Cross in Birmingham—paid particular attention to the maintenance of streets. By the middle of the sixteenth century, however, this mechanism, which had always been haphazard, became unworkable. Many of the manorial courts had ceased to be effective; land, and the responsibilities that went with its ownership, changed hands with bewildering rapidity at the time as a consequence of the Dissolution of the Monasteries; in the reign of Edward VI the chantries were dissolved, and with them the majority of the charitable gilds. The Act of 1555 declared, once and for all, that the liability for maintaining roads rested with the parishes through which they ran. If the parishioners neglected their duty in this regard, they could be indicted at Quarter Sessions and fined. This was not a new principle, for the common law had long recognised such an obligation. But it was now made statutory, and a new method was adopted for its enforcement. In future, Surveyors of Highways were to be elected annually by the parishioners; and four (later six) days in the year were to be appointed during which the parishioners should give their labour or that of hired substitutes for the repair of the roads, under the Surveyors' direction.

The duties of the Surveyors were onerous and disagreeable. Three times a year they were required to view the whole parish and testify before a magistrate to the state of the roads and bridges. They were responsible for presenting any of their fellow-parishioners who transgressed the provisions of the Act, either by failing to provide labour or by obstructing the highways or by using more animals for draught than the Act allowed. Not surprisingly, the Surveyors' office was an unpopular one.

This measure was far from perfect. The Surveyors had no technical skill in the work that was thrust upon them and were subject to all kinds of personal and social inducement to neglect the full performance of their duties. William Harrison complained in the 1570s that 'albeit that the intent of the statute is very profitable for the reparations of the decayed places, yet the rich do so cancel their portions and the poor so loiter in their labours that of all the six scarcely two good days' works were well performed'; adding the further criticism that the Surveyors often selected for repair the roads that were of personal interest to them and that the owners of the stone needed for repairing the roads profiteered in its sale.[17]

Nevertheless, the Act of 1555 marks an important stage in the history of transport in England. It represented a simple and intelligible instrument for the maintenance of the country's road system. In the very long run, its working depended not so much on the energy or evasiveness of individual Surveyors as on the pressure that could be brought to bear on them by those who needed to use the roads.

That the principles embodied in the Act were found correct at the time is evident. Its operation was limited to seven years. When that experimental period was up in 1562 it was renewed; and in 1586 another Act was passed, which stated that the previous measures had been 'found to be very necessary and profitable for the common wealth of this realm' and accordingly made their provisions permanent. The system thus established was modified in two important respects in 1691. The appointment of Surveyors was then taken out of the hands of the parishioners and given to Quarter Sessions; and the parishes were authorised, if they chose, to levy rates for the repair of highways, the proceeds to be applied to hiring labour —a more efficient method than that of exacting labour from the parishioners themselves. In its main principles, however, the Tudor legislation lasted for the better part of three centuries, until it was swept away by the Highways Act of 1835.[18]

At the same time numerous efforts were made, by Government and the courts, to keep the highways in repair through restriction of loads and control of the vehicles that carried them. Kent Quarter Sessions in 1604 heard a complaint that loads had of late much increased: whereas in former years carts had seldom carried more than one ton, now their loads were reaching two tons and a half, 'whereby the highway from Canterbury to Sittingbourne is thereby spoiled to the great annoyance of all travellers'. It was therefore ordered that the owner of any cart carrying a load exceeding one ton should pay five shillings 'to be bestowed in and upon the amendment of the said highways'.[19] This was a more intelligent method of dealing with the problem than that adopted by the royal Government, which issued proclamations in 1621 and 1629 entirely forbidding the carriage of loads exceeding one ton. They were quite ineffective.

Another means of achieving the same end was to restrict the number of horses that might be used to haul a single load. The Highways Act of 1662 limited it to seven. It also required that all carts should have wheels not less than four inches wide, in the belief that narrow wheels cut deeper and more dangerous ruts in the road: a matter on which there was endless argument for a century and more to come.

All this regulation of road transport had one very marked characteristic. Its purpose was conservative, to maintain the existing system in repair. It did nothing to help new construction, either of roads or of bridges. The task of conservation was difficult enough; and we cannot be surprised that the object of all authorities, central and local, was to keep the roads usable by enforcing the legislation for their maintenance and at the same time restricting the demands that might be made upon them. This was a policy that could succeed only at a time of economic stagnation or decline. It was destroyed by the expansion of trade and the complication of its techniques under Elizabeth and the Stuarts. Better transport facilities were now required, and in the end the traders were strong enough to get them.

Trade and industrial activity expanded greatly in Elizabethan England: in iron and brass work, in the making of woollens and sugar and soap, in new manufactures like the cottons of Manchester and old ones, like the cutlery of Sheffield, that achieved new fame abroad. A similar, though more modest, expansion is to be seen in Wales, especially in the development of its mineral resources. Wales, too, was now being drawn into a closer connection with the English economy. London merchants and shipowners were becoming increasingly interested in Welsh trade. A great man like Sir Henry Sidney controlled, with his commercial associates, ironworks both in Glamorgan and in the Weald of Sussex, linked by ships plying between Cardiff and Rye.[20]

But the most spectacular development was in coal production. Between 1563 and 1609 the shipments at Newcastle multiplied seven times over. The coalfield of Northumberland and Durham continued to be the biggest in Britain, and almost the whole of its produce was transported by sea: in English ships by this time, not in foreigners'. In 1600 Queen Elizabeth incorporated the Company of Hostmen of Newcastle, giving it a control both over the municipal government and over the economic life of Tyneside that it retained until the eighteenth century. The Company was entrusted with the exclusive right to ship coal from Tyneside, paying duty to the Crown for the privilege on every shipment. The vessels that took part in this trade were much the largest British ships engaged in coastal work, and during the seventeenth century they grew constantly larger still. In 1606 the average coal cargo brought into London was 73 tons; by the end of the century it was nearly four times as big. The total import of coal into London from the Tyne in 1702 was 180,000 tons. The east-coast ports—notably Scarborough at this time—had a predominant share in the English coastal trade, and the staple of it was coal.[21]

Yet in the seventeenth century more coal was being marketed by land than by water. In the most populous part of Great Britain, southern England, no coal was then worked, save in Somerset. But in all the other districts of greatest population—the Midlands and Lancashire, Yorkshire and the North-East, eastern and central Scotland—the deposits of coal were widely distributed and abundant. One of the richest fields, that in Warwickshire, lay close to the Roman Watling Street and Foss Way, which were both used by trains of packhorses from the collieries. Some of this coal went to a considerable distance. In 1581 the tenants of the Brudenells were hauling coal from Coleorton in the Leicestershire field to Deene in Northamptonshire, some forty miles, as a rent service.[22]

At the same time the roads were also being used, to a much greater extent than before, for the conveyance of heavy miscellaneous goods by waggon. Carriers' services, running at regular intervals, appeared before the end of Elizabeth's reign: Ipswich had a thrice-weekly service to London in 1599. Less than forty years later, in 1637, John Taylor the Water-poet published a *Carriers Cosmography*, which enumerated the services then in operation between London and all parts of England, with the names of the London inns to and from which they ran.

The account that emerges from this little work is impressive. In his preface Taylor defends himself against the charge that numerous towns are omitted from his list by saying that 'if a carrier of York hath a letter or goods to deliver at any town on his way thither, he serves the town well enough, and there are carriers and messengers from York to carry such goods and letters as are to be passed any ways north, broad and wide as far or further than Berwick: so that he that sends to Hereford may from thence be passed to St. Davids in Wales, the Worcester carriers can convey anything as far as Carmarthen and those that go to Chester may send to Caernarvon: the carriers or posts that go to Exeter may send daily to Plymouth or to the Mount in Cornwall'. We must not take all this too literally. Taylor had a bombastic temperament, so that he inflated most things he touched, and his list is self-evidently a hasty compilation, in which repetitions and errors abound. Yet making all proper allowances, it is possible to say that the *Carriers Cosmography* reveals an organised system of goods transport. The very compilation of the pamphlet, by a publicist so expert as Taylor, is an indication of the demand for the kind of information it supplied.

The roads were thus coming to be burdened with much new and heavy traffic. They suffered seriously, too, in the seventeenth century from military operations. The campaigns of the Civil War, like most others of the time, were chiefly summer campaigns; for the moving of large bodies of troops, with their ammunition and equipment, over the roads as they then were would have been an impossible task in winter. Though the English Civil War was a more humane war than most, it left great destruction behind it. The King's army, marching across Worcestershire in 1644, was said to have done such damage to the bridges that it would cost the county £10,000 to repair them; and they suffered further in the campaign of 1651. At the Somerset Quarter Sessions at Bridgwater in October 1646 a general complaint was made of 'the defect in several bridges occasioned

18

by the marching of armies to and fro, whereby the county cannot have recourse from one place to another but by other unusual ways and that many times with hazard'. It was accordingly determined that all the county bridges should be put into repair. One may doubt if the work was undertaken quickly.[23]

The Civil War and the political upheaval that followed it had another effect on transport and travel in Britain which was more lasting. They stimulated the desire for a better knowledge of the country's transport system. Again we must trace the origins of this back to the sixteenth century, when foreign travellers came frequently to this island, on business or from curiosity, and described what they saw: Frenchmen like Etienne Perlin and the Duc de Rohan, who visited their country's traditional ally Scotland as well as her traditional enemy England, Paul Hentzner the German, Thomas Platter from Switzerland.[24] At the same time Englishmen were themselves becoming conscious of what was worth seeing in parts of the country that were unfamiliar to them: such as Fynes Moryson, whose *Itinerary* was published in 1617 though based chiefly on journeys made in the 1590s, and the three army officers who made a rapid summer jaunt on horseback through England in 1634.[25] Travellers like these needed maps and guide-books to help them, and they now began to be supplied. The county maps of Saxton and Speed were satisfactory for consultation in a library but hardly portable by the traveller on horseback; nor did they give him all the information he wanted in planning a journey. Their contemporary, John Norden, did more for him. He made maps of some ten English counties, on which he delineated the main roads; and in 1625 he produced *An Intended Guide for English Travellers*, which comprised triangular distance tables, of a pattern that was apparently his invention and has continued in use ever since ⟨42⟩. This little book was followed ten years later by the anonymous *Direction for the English Traveller, By which he Shall be enabled to Coast about all England and Wales And also to know how far any Market or other notable Town in any Shire lieth one from another*. Norden's distance tables were incorporated in this work. It was a successful publication, reissued in 1636 and three times in 1643. These last issues seem to have been produced in response to a demand by officers of the Parliamentarian army in London for a guide to be used on their campaigns. The same publisher, Thomas Jenner, commissioned Wenceslaus Hollar to engrave a *Quartermaster's Map*, designed specifically for military purposes, in 1644.[26]

One consequence of the Civil War was to give a large number of men who served in the opposing armies some knowledge of parts of Britain that were hitherto unknown to them: a consequence little noticed, yet important in enlarging their minds' horizons. (Much the same enlargement took place

19

during the World Wars of the twentieth century, which showed thousands of Englishmen countries overseas that they would never have visited for themselves and gave them, in some measure, a new curiosity and a wider outlook.) The English conquest of Scotland, moreover, and Cromwell's short-lived effort towards a political unification of Britain, imparted to those old antagonists a new knowledge of each other: expressed for instance in Thomas Tucker's interesting survey of the Scottish ports, made for the Commissioners of Excise in 1655.[27]

Most of these travellers' journeys were made on horseback. But coaches were now coming into common use. Though what the Elizabethans called 'chariots or whirlicotes' were known in the Middle Ages, they were used only by delicate women or invalids, and even they preferred, for smoothness, to travel by water or in a litter or portable bed. Coaches, as we know them, were introduced into Britain about the middle of the sixteenth century, and by the end of Elizabeth's reign they were owned by a fair number of nobles and gentlemen. The Queen herself may have had one or two but usually rode on horseback or was carried in a litter. Thomas Platter hired one for his travels, but the coachman (who had himself hired it from a peer), having driven him from London to Oxford, flatly refused to take him on to Cambridge. His grounds were that one wheel of the coach had already been damaged and that 'the road was too boggy and difficult to find, for that neighbourhood was uninhabited and rather deserted'; and he was upheld in his refusal by the Oxford smiths, who were called on for an opinion. These vehicles were at once cumbrous and fragile.

None the less they multiplied, to the scandal of the old-fashioned and the envious. 'The world runs on wheels with many,' wrote Stow in his *Survey of London*, 'whose parents were glad to go on foot.' An attempt to restrict their use was made in Parliament in 1601, it being alleged that they took up so many horses that the Government would be unable to get those it needed for the army; but it failed. Satirists might poke fun at them, like Stephen Gosson, who wrote of the 'upstart newfangled gentlewomen' who rode in them:

> To carry all this pelf and trash,
> Because their bodies are unfit,
> Our wantons now in coaches dash
> From house to house, from street to street. . . .
> As poorer trulls must ride in carts,
> So coaches are for prouder hearts.

It was all to no purpose. Most people of substance quickly came to own them. Even the tough Martin Frobisher, whom no one could call effeminate,

20

had two to dispose of in his will when he died in 1595. Twenty years later Fynes Moryson wrote that there were so many coaches that 'the streets of London are almost stopped up with them'. Ten years more, and a new phenomenon had appeared: the hackney coach,* to be hired by anybody in London.

This development at once aroused furious opposition from the Thames watermen, who had hitherto had the monopoly of conveying passengers from one part of London to another. They were a powerful body—first organised, as we have seen, in the reigns of Henry VIII and Mary—subject to regulations made by the Lord Mayor, not unlike those governing taxi-men today though on some points more stringent. A set made in 1583, for example, prescribes a penalty of up to a month's imprisonment and a five-shilling fine for watermen who 'do fight, brawl, chide or give evil words' and forbids them to ask more than their fixed fares or to 'lay hands upon any person to draw him contrary to his will to come to their boats'. These rules also provide for the payment of a small pension to watermen past work.[28] Such a well-developed corporation would obviously not submit to the competition of a new and dangerous rival without a fierce struggle. Its most effective propagandist was John Taylor, who devoted much energy to the defence of his calling as a waterman and the blackening of hackney coachmen: 'this infernal swarm of trade-spillers, who like the grasshoppers or caterpillars of Egypt have so over-run the land that we can get no living upon the water'.[29] The Government repeatedly sought to control them by limiting their number—to 50 in 1637, to 300 in 1654, to 400 in 1662; but the demand for more coaches was insatiable, reflecting the continual expansion of London, and the mounting wealth of its citizens. Sedan chairs also appeared at the same time, to be used especially by women ⟨35⟩. Though strong rivalry continued between these conflicting interests, there was in fact plenty of work for watermen, coachmen, and chairmen alike for a century and more to come.

By this time the use of the coach was beginning to develop in another direction too, which was even more important for the future. In the *Carriers Cosmography* of 1637 Taylor tells us that a weekly coach conveyed passengers between London and St. Albans. Ten years later a regular service was in operation between Rochester and Gravesend, in connection with the boats that plied up the Thames to London. In 1649 the term 'stage coaches' made its appearance in Chamberlayne's *Present State of Great Britain*, which observed that they were then running from London 'to the principal towns of the country . . . at the low price of about a shilling for every five miles'. It is hard to disbelieve this circumstantial

* The name had nothing to do with the parish of Hackney. It was derived from the Middle English word *hakenai*, an ambling horse suitable for ladies to ride on.

statement; yet puzzling that if it is correct so little more is heard of these coaches for some time. In 1658 we suddenly find services being advertised, mostly on three days in the week, from London to Exeter and Plymouth; to Chester and Kendal; to Wakefield, York, and Newcastle; and (a flash in the pan, surely, during Cromwell's union with Scotland) 'once every fortnight to Edinburgh for £4 apiece'. After the Restoration these services multiplied, and in 1669 an effort was made to maintain one running at exceptionally high speed in the 'flying coach' that completed the journey from Oxford to London in a single day of thirteen hours, or at an average speed of between four and five miles an hour.

Side by side with these coaches, and travelling faster, went the royal posts on horseback. In Elizabeth's reign five great post roads—to Dover, to Berwick and Carlisle, to North Wales, to South Wales, and to Cornwall—were divided into regular stages, at each of which horses were maintained for forwarding the post and for the use of travellers bearing commissions from the Queen. In 1635, through the work of Thomas Withering and Sir John Coke, a much more highly developed system was established, with by-posts from the main roads and a series of charges, varied according to distance, from twopence for a letter going up to eighty miles to eightpence for one addressed to Scotland. Though the Civil War destroyed these arrangements, the republican Government revived them, and they formed the foundation of the permanent system that was developed in the 1660s. By that time the mail normally took just over two full days to reach Plymouth or Chester, and not more than five days to Edinburgh. In 1680 a London Penny Post was set up by a private citizen, William Dockwra. He quickly lost control of it on the ground that he was infringing the patent of the Duke of York, on whom the profits of the Post Office had been settled by Parliament; but the innovation was too useful to be suppressed.

For many purposes, then, the roads came to be more heavily used in the seventeenth century. The new wheeled vehicles, which were ponderous and springless, jolted along them slowly and with great discomfort to their passengers. When, like that Oxford coach, they attempted speed, the journey must have been a gruesome experience. Such developments made nonsense of the principles laid down in the Highways Act of 1555 and its successors. For the burden of maintaining roads fell most inequitably. The inhabitants of parishes lying on much-frequented highways naturally felt that they were being taxed for the benefit of carriers and passengers from a distance: like those of Bedminster, who complained that their roads were 'much impaired and decayed by reason of the great carriage towards the city of Bristol', and those of Marden in Kent who said with equally good reason that their roads were ruined 'by the much carrying of great guns and timber' at the outbreak of the third Dutch War in 1672.[30] To such complaints were added those of countless parishes that were traversed by the great trunk roads.

Among them none were more unfortunate than those lying athwart the Great North Road to the north of Royston. One of them, Radwell, petitioned the Government for help in 1656, stating that whatever repairs were effected in summer were all undone in winter. Quite evidently, the task was beyond the resources of the few inhabitants of the place. The state of this road remained notorious, and in 1663 an Act was passed for repairing that part of it lying within the counties of Hertford, Cambridge, and Huntingdon, which asserted an important new principle. In each of these counties a gate was to be erected across the road at which every drove of cattle or sheep, every vehicle and every horseman, was to pay a fixed toll. The money so collected was to be spent, under the direction of Surveyors appointed by the Justices, on the repair of the road. The Act therefore recognised that the practice laid down in 1555 was no longer applicable to roads carrying heavy traffic. It stated, in effect, that those who used the road must help to pay for its upkeep. The Act was not successful, for some travellers evaded the gates, and the revenue from tolls was disappointing; it was even allowed to lapse for a time. But it was not altogether forgotten, and when a similar problem arose over the road between London, Colchester, and Harwich, another measure on the same lines was passed to deal with it in 1695–96.

We are fortunate indeed to have an excellent account of all the main roads and the principal cross roads in England and Wales in John Ogilby's *Britannia* of 1675 ⟨44⟩: the first detailed set of road maps for this country, and of such merit that they continued as the basis of all others for over a century. Ogilby and his assistants perambulated the roads with a 'way-wiser' ⟨43⟩, and he claimed, with justifiable pride, that his survey was based on 'actual dimensuration'. It was indeed astonishingly accurate, as one can tell by comparing it with the modern Ordnance Survey map: a simple exercise, as he used throughout a scale of one inch to a mile.

It would be wrong to suggest that the whole energy and inventiveness of the seventeenth century was directed into road transport. Other efforts, no less energetic, were made to improve the navigation of rivers. Indeed, if we distinguish rigidly between river navigation and wholly artificial canals, the years between 1600 and 1750 saw 'the greatest attempt to improve the rivers of England and to use them as means of communication that has ever been made in the country's history'.[31]

Something that can be correctly called a canal had been built in Elizabeth's reign, in 1564–66: the Exeter Canal, nearly three miles long, which enabled boats to by-pass the weirs of the lower Exe and made

C

Exeter once again what it had been three centuries before, a port in its own right, independent of Topsham. This work was important in the history of British engineering because it made use of pound locks: locks of the kind we are most familiar with, in which the boat is lowered or raised on the water by being enclosed within a chamber formed by a pair of lock gates with movable sluices. Though such locks had been in use in the Low Countries for a long time past, they had not been seen previously in Britain. They were more economical of water than the old flash-locks, and very much safer; but since, on the other hand, they were more expensive to construct and slower in operation, they did not rapidly supersede the older type.

The Exeter Canal was not very successful at first, since it was too shallow and Exeter quay too small. It was a hundred years before the quay was enlarged and the handsome custom-house built that still symbolises the city's status as a port ⟨106⟩, and the canal needed substantial extension and dredging in 1676 and 1698–1701. It exercised no important influence on those who were concerned with the development of inland navigation in the seventeenth century. Apart from a few visionaries, they interested themselves solely in the improvement of the existing rivers.

Some such improvement had, as we have seen, taken place in the later Middle Ages. In the sixteenth century it was carried a little further, eight Acts of Parliament being passed then for this purpose. Among them was one of 1571 for the improvement of the Lea, primarily for the benefit of London. The work was carried out within the next ten years, and it gave rise to controversy, litigation, even violence. It was opposed by some of the inhabitants of 'the decayed town of Enfield', which attributed its decay to the new navigation. In the past Enfield had been an *entrepôt* for corn and barley on its way from the Midlands to London, and its carriers complained that they were now ruined. They probably did suffer loss, even if it was less serious than they made out: for it is a recurring theme in this story that the re-routing of transport, if it benefits one community, will almost certainly disadvantage another. The whole tale, with its argument and counter-argument, is characteristic of the history of these undertakings. It is also characteristic of the time that Burghley himself should have investigated it (in September 1588, the Armada crisis barely over), laboriously compiling notes of the loads carried by the Lea barges, the tolls taken, the wages of the bargemen and the time they took to get from Bow Bridge to Waltham and Ware; and that in the Star Chamber the rights and wrongs of the case should have had to be disentangled by the two Chief Justices of England.[32]

Both under Elizabeth and under the Stuarts the Government sometimes went to great pains to settle questions of this sort rightly. In the trouble-some case of the projected improvement of the River Lark from Bury St. Edmunds to Mildenhall in 1635–38, Charles I's Privy Council earnestly tried to achieve a solution that was in the true public interest. It insisted, for example, on a demonstration of the comparative costs of transport by land and by water: the soundest possible basis on which to assess the merits of the plan.

Not much was done for river navigation under the first two Stuarts or during the Interregnum. The Corporation of Bath secured rights to improve the River Avon to Bristol in 1619, but it did nothing active in the matter. Thomas Skipwith, granted a patent in 1634 to improve the River Soar from Leicester to the Trent, began work on a few miles at the north end and then abandoned it for want of capital. Something effective was done in the 1630s by William Sandys on the Warwickshire Avon and by John Mallett on the Tone, which he improved between Bridgwater and Ham Mill, three miles east of Taunton. The Wey was made navigable from Guildford to the Thames in 1651–53.

The last 40 years of the seventeenth century brought two great bursts of interest in river navigation. Nine Acts of Parliament were passed for this purpose in 1662–65, and eight more in 1697–1700. Many different economic pressures combined to cause this great activity. The increasing demand for coal was one of the most important. This was the main argu-ment put forward for the improvement of the Salisbury Avon in 1664–65 and the Tone in 1698. The north-country clothiers of Kendal, Leeds, and Wakefield supported the first Aire and Calder navigation Bill in the same year, in the confidence that if the scheme were carried through it would lower their costs considerably. There was never any difficulty in proving that it was cheaper to send goods by water than by land. The opponents of this Bill conceded that the cost of carrying cloth 25 miles overland from Leeds to York was four times as great as that of taking it over the 50 miles from York down the Ouse to Hull. Many individual supporters of these navigations looked to them to increase the value of their property. Lord Paget, for example, who was much concerned with the improvement of the Trent in 1699, was lord of the manor of Burton and deeply interested in the development of the Staffordshire coalfield. (So deeply that some of his lessees presented him, in gratitude, with his coat of arms cut in coal, which he set up in his gallery at Beaudesert.)

These undertakings were financed in several different ways. If the money was found by municipal corporations, they raised it from taxes or by a loan. Both methods were followed by the city of Oxford in its efforts to improve the navigation of the Thames in 1635–59. The Act for the improvement of the Colne (1698) made the Corporation of Colchester responsible for the work, with permission to raise the £4,000 needed by mortgaging the tolls at 6 per cent interest for 21 years. The navigation of the Wye and Lugg was undertaken by three members of the Sandys family, who were authorised to levy a substantial sum from the county of Hereford for the purpose. It was often difficult to secure the required capital; no one drew great profits from investing in river navigations.

Yet if the task of extending them was laborious, the work went steadily on. By the end of the seventeenth century the system of river navigation in England totalled about 1,000 miles. Very few districts that could be described as populous lay, by this time, more than 15 miles from navigable water. The outlines of a national system of water transport were beginning to emerge.

Turnpikes and Canals

ALTHOUGH THE PRINCIPLE adopted for the repair of part of the Great North Road in 1663 did not work out satisfactorily at first and was not imitated elsewhere for 30 years, it suddenly gained rapid acceptance after 1700. This was partly due to the great success achieved by the second operation of this kind, on the main road to Harwich. 'These roads were formerly deep,' wrote Defoe, 'in time of floods dangerous, and at other times, in winter, scarce passable; they are now so firm, so safe, so easy to travellers, and carriages as well as cattle, that no road in England can yet be said to equal them; this was first done by the help of a turnpike, set up by Act of Parliament, about the year 1697, at a village near Ingatestone'.[33] The word 'turnpike', to denote the barrier fixed across the road at the point at which payment was demanded, first occurs in 1678. As these barriers became more numerous, the term passed into common use, until eventually it came to mean the road itself, as it still does in the United States.

Some 400 Acts of Parliament were passed for the improvement of particular stretches of road by this method in the first half of the eighteenth century: the greatest number for the south-east of England, the smallest for the far north, none at all for Scotland, for North Wales, or for the three counties of Dorset, Devon, and Cornwall. This reflects their economic backwardness at this time, for the advantages that followed a well-executed turnpike scheme were considerable. They cheapened the carriage of goods, in spite of the tolls that had to be paid, since the improved going enabled

26

the horses to draw heavier loads at higher speeds, and cattle driven to market on the hoof, as Defoe put it, 'drive lighter, and come to market with less toil, and consequently both go farther in one day, and not waste their flesh, and heat and spoil themselves, in wallowing through the mud and sloughs, as is now the case'. Bridges, too, were multiplying in place of the old fords, which were often impassable: Defoe instances a series of eleven new bridges between Southwark and Croydon, 'by which the whole road is laid dry, sound, and hard, which was before a most uncomfortable road to travel'. And that leads him to emphasise a social consequence of the improvement of roads: the expansion of the radius of the suburbs, within which citizens could now live and make their daily journeys on business into London.[34]

The administration of the turnpike roads was at first entrusted to the county magistrates. But this was not a satisfactory expedient, since they already had a multitude of other duties and many of them took no interest in this new one. In 1706 a fresh experiment was tried, that of naming a body of trustees to look after a single stretch of road; and this came to be the accepted pattern ⟨46⟩.

The principles underlying the establishment of these trusts were simple. They were first thought of as a device for remedying a temporary defect in one section of a road. It was assumed that when the money from the tolls had been spent the work of improvement would be complete. The powers given to the trusts were therefore limited in time, usually to 21 years. It soon became invariable practice, however, for Parliament to renew them and so the trusts became, in fact though never in theory, permanent. The authority of each was limited to its own stretch of road; and though at first these stretches were long—the earliest Act of 1663 applied to nearly 70 miles of the Great North Road—they were soon drastically shortened. Between 1707 and 1727 seven Acts were passed establishing turnpike roads in Wiltshire. The average length brought under each was nine miles. In 1727 a further Act set up a turnpike trust for a group of roads radiating from Warminster, none of which exceeded four miles in length.[35]

This was an unsatisfactory feature of the system. Since the units were so small the great trunk roads came quickly to resemble a patchwork quilt, with one short stretch turnpiked and the next unimproved. The Government left the whole initiative in establishing turnpike trusts to the local inhabitants. There was therefore no authority strong enough to insist that equal attention should be given to the whole road.

Nor was this the only defect of the new arrangements. The finance of the trusts was open to much criticism. The collection of the tolls was arbitrary, since numerous exemptions were allowed in all the Acts. Later in the century it became usual for the trustees to farm out the tolls to the highest bidder at a public auction; and the knaveries of the toll-farmers and their employees the 'pikemen', who collected the tolls at the gates, were notorious. Nor were the trustees above suspicion. The Kensington trust, with a revenue of more than twice what was needed to keep the 15 miles of its road in repair, was £3,300 in debt in 1749; and there was still gross mismanagement of this important road in 1765. Treasurers sometimes absconded with the funds in their charge, and an attempt was made in 1755 to see that turnpike trustees should in future be men of substance, who might be presumed to be less open to such temptations than small farmers or shopkeepers.

The most serious defect of all, however, in the early turnpike trusts was not inefficient administration or financial malpractice. It was inadequate engineering skill. When the trusts were first established, almost nothing was known of the science of making a road fit to carry continuous and heavy-wheeled traffic, in summer and winter alike. A few treatises on road-making had been written in the seventeenth century; Robert Phillips published a *Dissertation concerning the Present State of the High Roads of England* in 1737, very sensible on metalling and quite wrong-headed about drainage: but such works were little studied. The methods adopted were drawn from the traditional lore of the parish Surveyors and, slowly and painfully, from experiment.

The more energetic turnpike trusts tried out different techniques of road-making. It was generally agreed that the surface should be convex, to keep the crown dry and to allow water to drain away at the sides. But even this principle was not universally adhered to. William Marshall noted with disapproval that some Midland roads were made in the form of a 'trough', and he recorded a costly experiment on the three-mile stretch of road from London to Hackney, which was altered from 'the *barrel* to the *wave* form' in the hope that artificial ruts would improve the drainage, and then had to be remade to its original pattern. He also remarked on the vast improvement effected in a notoriously bad length of road between Tamworth and Ashby-de-la-Zouch by the application of sand to it, in a layer 18 in.–2 ft. deep. His definition of the perfect road was that its surface should be 'moderately round, with a free open channel on either side as a horse path; with banks level on the top, as guards to the paths, and as resources, in wet weather, for foot-passengers; and, where the width of the lane will permit, with a side road for summer travelling'.[36]

Marshall was only one of the many busy writers on agriculture who devoted attention to roads as an important factor in the proper exploitation of the land. One of his fellows, Arthur Young, has been constantly quoted, from his own time to ours, for his vehement denunciation of the roads he travelled on in many parts of England. He is indeed eminently quotable. 'From Grimsthorpe to Colsterworth,' he writes, 'are eight miles, called by the courtesy of the neighbourhood a turnpike, but in which we were every moment either buried in quagmires of mud or racked to dislocation over pieces of rock which they term *mending*.' Or again, 'I know not, in the whole range of language, terms sufficiently expressive to describe this infernal road [from Preston to Wigan]. Let me most seriously caution all travellers who may accidentally purpose to travel this terrible country, to avoid it as they would the devil; for a thousand to one but they break their necks or their limbs by overthrows or breakings-down.'[37]

This may have been fair comment on these particular roads. But are Young's judgments on this matter in general to be trusted? Was he a dispassionate and reliable observer? The answer is 'no'. He was an enthusiast, a perfectionist, whether he was pursuing his ideas about crops or the management of farms or about the political economy of England. There was a trace of hysteria in his temperament. And moreover he was constantly pressed for time, turning the accounts of his travels into bread and butter. Any delay was liable to put him into a passion. Other travellers, his contemporaries, give us a different impression of the English roads. Pennant, travelling from Chester to London in 1780, looked back to his boyhood forty years earlier when he made the journey by stage coach in six long days, dragged through the bad patches of road by six or eight horses. 'The single gentlemen, then a hardy race, equipped in jack-boots and trousers up to their middle, rode post through thick and thin, and, guarded against the mire, defied the frequent stumble and fall; arose and pursued their journey with alacrity: while in these days their enervated posterity sleep away their rapid journeys in easy chaises, fitted for the conveyance of the soft inhabitants of Sybaris.'[38] Foreign visitors looked at English roads with envy. In the 1720s De Saussure described them as 'magnificent, being wide, smooth, and well kept', and attributed their good quality to the turnpike system. Count Friedrich von Kielmansegge, coming over from Hanover to attend the coronation of George III in 1761, was astonished at the smooth ease of travelling from Harwich to London and at the speed attainable in a post-chaise on the Bath road. The Frenchman De St. Fond was lyrical in his praise of the Great North Road in 1784, and though when he ventured into the Highlands of Scotland he found travelling perilous, he noted with strong approval the excellence of the highways round Edinburgh.[39]

As one reviews the accounts given by these travellers and many more, one is obliged to recognise that a great general improvement in the condition of the main roads of England was brought about in the course of the eighteenth century; and this improvement extended gradually to Wales and Scotland. With little exaggeration it has been said of Scotland that 'nothing wrought so remarkable a change in civilising the country, in developing its trade, and improving the social and industrial condition of the people, as the Turnpike Road Act of 1791'.[40] It was not only a matter of repairing and maintaining the roads: they were made increasingly convenient to the traveller. Signposts had begun to appear in the seventeenth century. Now they multiplied fast, many of them giving information about distances and stating the name of the parish in which they were situated ⟨49⟩. Sir Francis Dashwood even erected a land lighthouse in 1751: the Dunston Pillar, which bore a light to guide the traveller over the wild heathland south of Lincoln ⟨48⟩. Such assistance was always welcome, for as John Byng constantly noted it was difficult to get any accurate information about the country from the people of the place. Wishing to go from Gloucester to Monmouth, he found that 'every one agreed in the distance, and that the road was intolerably bad, but nobody had travelled it or could give me the least information; the first person met in Piccadilly could tell more of the country than I could learn in the Bell Inn at Gloucester'. As he wrote, with disillusionment, in 1790: 'I travel by map, for none can inform you; the only people who become acquainted with counties are tourists or a canvasser at a general election.'[41] For such travellers as he, maps and guide-books were produced in increasing numbers: notably the road-books of Cary and Paterson, which ran steadily through edition after edition from 1771 to 1832 ⟨66⟩.

At the same time the business of inn-keeping was greatly extended, and the inns themselves grew in grandeur, like the White Hart at Salisbury ⟨74⟩ or the Swan at Bedford, designed by Henry Holland to the Duke of Bedford's instructions. The food and service the inns offered frequently left much to be desired; yet they afforded, to those who could pay their sometimes extortionate charges, a generally reliable national service, and they made possible the growth of the modern tourist industry.

It was now that the very word 'tourist' began to come into use[42]—in half-mocking tones, indicating that a tour was itself something of an absurdity. People began to visit wild parts of the country, North Wales and the Lakes and the Highlands, in pursuit of antiquities and of 'the picturesque'; and though they relished rugged scenery, they also wanted to travel in their accustomed comfort, by good roads, to stay at well-appointed inns. They did not get their wishes granted immediately; but they set in train a process carried much further in subsequent years, with the help of the steamer, the railway, and the motor-car.

Not every one approved of all this gadding round. Byng himself referred wryly to 'my own touring about and the eternal racket of the whole kingdom'.[43] Some people made it a matter of pride to resist the temptation and to remain stationary. In the parish church of Holyhead there is a monument to John Owen of Penrhos, who died in 1712 aged 84: 'a person', says his epitaph, 'who never having travelled for education beyond the circuit of his own native island yet by the singular felicity of his genius attained to such accomplishments as to be its greatest delight and ornament for wit, its chief oracle for civil prudence, a stranger to few parts of useful learning and . . . a great pattern of unaffected piety and devotion'. Whether 'his own native island' means, as it properly should, the tiny Holy Island, or whether it extends to Anglesey, the circuit of his life was small enough. A century later Richard Fenton—himself an experienced traveller, both as a lawyer on the Welsh Circuit and as an antiquary— reflected on the self-sufficient life led by his grandfather on his small estate of Manorowen in Pembrokeshire: 'Prior to the era of mail coaches, carriers, and waggons, and before a regular communication was opened by sea and land between the great marts of the kingdom and this remote corner of the island, the true *savoir vivre* consisted in having everything that contributed to the comfort of life, as much as possible within one's own reach, without being beholden to casualty for supplies.'[44] He was dependent for nothing, whether necessity or luxury, upon transport from the outside world.

*   *   *

The improvement of the roads that has been described in this chapter benefited the traveller greatly. There was room for further improvement still, and that began to appear before the eighteenth century was out; but, beyond question, it was much easier to move about Britain in 1780 than it had been in 1700. The trader, however, had gained less. Certainly, he did benefit from the change in one important respect. A quicker, more frequent and regular mail service sprang from the Post Office Act of 1711, which (following closely on the Union with Scotland) established for the first time a unified postal system for the whole of Great Britain under one Postmaster-General. Surveyors were appointed from 1715 with power to examine mail-bags and letter-bills on the road. Their operations did much to expose the frauds and increase the efficiency of country postmasters. From 1720 onwards Ralph Allen ⟨51⟩ held the farm of all the provincial mail services off the great main roads. He developed them with methodical and unremitting care until his death in 1764, contributing perhaps more than any other single man to the establishment of a genuinely national postal service. His profits from successive Post Office contracts were large; but no one should grudge him his fortune, for it was made directly in the public interest.

Under Allen's later mail contracts the most striking improvements effected were in the manufacturing districts. Birmingham secured a daily postal service in 1748; in 1761 new services were established from Newcastle to Whitehaven and across the Pennines from Halifax to Manchester. These changes were made under pressure put on the Post Office by the traders in manufacturing towns, anxious to increase the volume of their business.[45]

But this did nothing to facilitate the carriage of the traders' goods. Parcels and light packets could be conveyed by coach; heavier goods had still to be sent by the clumsy and dilatory stage-waggon. When a great tree or a large piece of machinery—a boiler or a cylinder of one of the new stationary steam engines that were now coming into use, for example— had to travel by road, it was necessary for it to be hauled by a train of horses: heavy and slow labour even in summer on a good eighteenth-century road, hardly feasible at all on a bad one in winter. If the goods to be carried were fragile they were likely to break on the ruts in the road's surface; and industry was much concerned at this time not only with new machinery but with delicate products like the porcelains of Derby and Staffordshire.

The manufacturers' answer to this problem was to make all possible use of water transport. They would go to great lengths to forward goods by coastal shipping. In 1775 the Horsehay Company, near Wellington in Shropshire, was sending pig-iron to Chester by carting it to the Severn, putting it on river-boats to Bristol and then on to ships sailing round the coast of Wales to bring it to Chester up the Dee: a journey of over 400 miles by water, involving two trans-shipments of cargo, to avoid one of 60 miles by land.[46]

Coal presented a similar problem, of much greater magnitude. The Northumberland and Durham coalfields continued to thrive on the coastal trade with London and the South, prices and shipments being controlled by two 'rings', of Tyne fitters and Thames lighter-men. Much coal was distributed by other inland rivers, especially by the Severn, the Trent, and some of those recently 'improved', like the Aire and Calder. Nevertheless the demand remained unsatisfied where the coalfield was not placed conveniently close to a navigable river. Liverpool, for example, was supplied with coal almost entirely from mines lying between Prescot and St. Helens, some ten miles inland. It came by cart or packhorse along a road that had been turnpiked, largely in order to facilitate this very traffic, in 1726. In 1753 the turnpike trustees put up their tolls, to pay for improvements in the road from Prescot to Warrington, and at the same time the mine-owners raised the price of coal. One consequence was an outbreak of rioting against the trustees; another, the decision of the

Common Council of Liverpool to set on foot a survey for making navigable the Sankey Brook, running down from St. Helens to the Mersey just below Warrington. In the event Henry Berry, the engineer appointed to undertake the work, decided not to improve the Brook but to cut a canal beside it, some ten miles long. Its opening in 1757 is a landmark, for it was the first substantial canal of the modern kind to be constructed in Britain ⟨127⟩.[47]

It was immediately followed by another, very much more celebrated and more important: the canal built at the expense of the third Duke of Bridgewater under powers granted by Parliament in 1759. Again its prime business was the transport of coal, from the mines owned by the Duke at Worsley to Manchester—already forming with its neighbour Salford a 'conurbation' of 20,000 people and growing fast through its textile manufactures. Unlike the Sankey Navigation, a modestly competent job, this was a great work of engineering. It involved the cutting of a tunnel at Worsley to take the canal into the mines themselves and the building of an aqueduct at Barton, 200 yds. long, carrying the canal at a height of nearly 40 ft. above the River Irwell. The credit for the whole achievement must be shared between three men: the Duke, his agent John Gilbert, and his engineer James Brindley. The canal was opened from Worsley to Stretford in 1761 and continued into Manchester soon afterwards. It was opposed by all the established transport concerns, the Mersey & Irwell Navigation and the turnpike trusts; but it beat them by the superior convenience of the services it offered.

The Duke's interest was not confined to the canal from Worsley to Manchester. In 1762 he secured further powers to link it, by means of a second canal, with the Mersey at Runcorn. And four years later two other groups of investors obtained Acts authorising the construction of a pair of canals connected with his: the Trent & Mersey, running from Wilden Ferry in Derbyshire to Preston Brook and so over half a dozen miles of the Duke's canal to Runcorn; and the Staffordshire & Worcestershire, branching out of this new canal at Great Haywood to run to Bewdley on the Severn. No wonder the Trent & Mersey proprietors proudly called their canal the Grand Trunk: for, with the two rivers it joined, it offered a continuous navigable waterway across the breadth of England. Among its most persistent and energetic supporters was Josiah Wedgwood, the growth of whose potteries was dependent on improved transport. He had subscribed £500 to local road improvements in 1765, and he acted as treasurer of the Grand Trunk Canal. His foresight was accurate. No one gained more than he did from the completion of the canal in 1777: it brought him his raw materials and dispersed his products smoothly and swiftly to the Severn, the Mersey, and the Humber.

33

Although the Staffordshire & Worcestershire was originally intended to run to Bewdley (a flourishing river-port, as we have seen, since the fifteenth century), the inhabitants of the town objected to the proposal, and the canal was diverted to reach the Severn four miles lower down, at the point of its junction with the Stour. On this site a mushroom town grew up, named Stourport. Very soon after the canal was opened in 1772 it eclipsed Bewdley as a place of trade. The older town continued to make a brave show, with a handsome new bridge over the Severn by Telford (1798), a promenade along the river, and a new town hall (1818). It remains a delightful place to visit now; but commercially it committed suicide about 1770. Although Stourport never grew large, it is bigger than Bewdley today. It takes its place with Goole as a town created by the development of inland water transport ⟨59–61⟩.

Birmingham was a much older place than Bewdley, and already a manufacturing town of importance. Yet it would hardly have grown into a great city without the canals that were cut into and through it in these years. The first, the Birmingham Canal, was a branch of the Staffordshire & Worcestershire, and was opened in the same year, 1772: the earliest built in this country as the feeder not to a navigable river but to another canal. Birmingham was quick to seize the potential advantages of its central position. Together with the Black Country, on its doorstep to the west, it became the hub of a wheel of canal communications, taking its products easily northwards to Lancashire and Yorkshire, westwards to Bristol, southwards to the Thames and London.

The chief canals of southern England were, naturally, focussed principally on the capital. The earliest of them was the Thames & Severn, tunnelling through the Cotswolds at Sapperton ⟨63⟩. A much greater work, also designed to link the Thames and Severn basins, was the Kennet & Avon, which ran from Newbury through Devizes to Bath ⟨93⟩. Most important of all was the Grand Junction, running from Brentford across the Chilterns at Tring to Napton in Warwickshire, where it joined the great Midland system. A branch was built from Hayes to a basin at Paddington, and this was extended by the Regent's Canal across North London to Limehouse on the Thames.

In South Wales the canals were an integral part of the development of the coalfield and they were linked, more intimately than anywhere else, with an extensive system of horse-tramroads that fed them and connected them together ⟨122⟩. There were no other canals of any importance elsewhere in Wales, except in the north-eastern corner of the country, where the Ellesmere and Montgomeryshire Canals connected Llangollen and Newton with the main system near Nantwich. The Ellesmere Canal, running through a steep and difficult country, entailed the construction of two

34

of the masterpieces of canal engineering, the aqueducts at Pontcysyllte and Chirk ⟨87–9⟩.

The object of all the chief northern canals was to cross the Pennines. The first to open up a satisfactory connection between Lancashire and Yorkshire was the Rochdale Canal, completed in 1804, followed by the Huddersfield (1811) and the Leeds & Liverpool (1816). The last of these was the greatest—the longest single line of canal ever constructed by one company in Britain—and it took 46 years to complete. Its course was circuitous, stretching in a great arc through Wigan, Burnley, and Skipton, crossing the main spine of hills at Foulridge near Colne. The distance between Leeds and Liverpool by canal was 127 miles, against 75 by road. But that was not a vital matter. For the carriage of heavy goods the canal was much safer and more convenient; and besides, on this canal, as on its rivals, the bulk of the traffic it carried proved to be local, stopping short on one side of the Pennines or the other.

The great canals of Scotland were three, all alike in some important respects and all different from those of England and Wales. They were designed as links between open seas. The first was the Forth & Clyde—a work that Defoe had urged early in the eighteenth century; begun in 1768, completed to Glasgow in 1775 and to the Clyde at Bowling near Dumbarton in 1790. Until the development of railways it carried a great trade, and it was a pioneer in the use of steamboats.

The second large Scottish undertaking was the Crinan Canal, across Knapdale, designed to cut out the long and stormy passage round the Mull of Kintyre and to bring the Western Islands into closer touch with Glasgow and the mainland. It took eight years to build (1793–1801) and it did not succeed, chiefly because the capital subscribed was inadequate to enable the work to be carried out properly. As the canal was not more than 10 ft. deep, it could take only small ships; it had too many locks; and the way out of it on the western side was inconvenient and dangerous.

Lastly, the Caledonian Canal: the most splendid project of the three, and a spectacular failure. Telford planned it to run through the Great Glen with a depth of 20 ft., enough to enable it to take substantial ships, which would thus be spared the fierce passage round Caithness and Sutherland. It was begun in 1803 and opened in 1822 for ships of a draught no greater than 12 ft. Though it was subsequently enlarged it never completely fulfilled its original purpose: not through any failure on Telford's part, nor through the parsimony of successive Governments, but because in the very years of its building the development of steam navigation rendered it unnecessary ⟨94⟩. A well-found steamship could weather the seas off the north coast of Scotland with little of the danger and delay to which sailing-ships had been exposed in the past.

35

All the great Scottish canals were in a sense State enterprises. The Caledonian Canal was financed entirely by the Government; the Crinan repeatedly borrowed from the Treasury and became national property in 1848; the completion of the Forth & Clyde in 1784–90 was made possible only by a Government loan. In England, little State aid was forthcoming: nor was much required. The great burst of canal construction in 1755–74 was experimental and it brought profits to investors who took long views, like the Duke of Bridgewater. In the succeeding years the works already sanctioned were carried through, some very slowly, and the crisis of the American War further delayed them. When peace returned, however, the country's mounting industrial production guaranteed the canals great profits. Year after year in the late eighties the Staffordshire & Worcestershire was paying over 20 per cent to its shareholders; the Birmingham company paid 23 per cent in 1789. In 1791–96 there was a boom in canal promotion: 51 new canals were authorised by Parliament, with a capital exceeding £7,600,000. Much money was made as well as lost in this feverish speculation, and when it was over the new companies that meant business had to construct their canals under adverse conditions, owing to the rising prices of the war against France. Thus the Kennet & Avon, authorised in 1794, moved forward at a snail's pace. In 1800 shares of over £50,000 were forfeited because their holders refused to pay the calls on them, and nobody would buy them at any price. It was opened at length in 1810, having cost a million pounds, or twice what was envisaged in 1794. It began to pay dividends in 1812, and over the next 30 years their rate averaged $6\frac{1}{4}$ per cent. Compare the Oxford Canal, whose construction was finished, in relatively cheap times, by 1790. Over the same period its average dividend was $31\frac{1}{2}$ per cent.[48]

What were the economic effects of the development of canals? It is not easy to give a general answer to that question. Beyond doubt they did much to cheapen the carriage of heavy goods: an analysis of a fair sample of the available evidence suggests that the cost of conveyance by canal was, on average, about a third of that of conveyance by road.[49] Yet other things must be taken into account. The total cost of transport would rise substantially if there was a long haul from the pit or factory to the water. And although it was undoubtedly cheaper to convey goods by water than by land, the price paid was fixed—sometimes within limits imposed by Parliament—at the discretion of the canal owners. If they exercised in effect a monopolistic control, that might keep prices high. In spite of the promise made by the promoters of the Sankey Navigation in 1754, the price of coal in Liverpool was 15–20 per cent higher in 1771; and it did not escape notice that the canal shareholders were then receiving a dividend of 20 per cent. The traders of Loughborough, who were also shareholders in the Soar Navigation, used their position to keep prices artificially high in Leicester from 1778 until the opening of the Leicester Navigation in 1794.[50] In other words, the cutting of a canal did not of necessity mean a lowering of freight charges. But it usually did; and this was a benefit felt equally by the manufacturer and by the consumer.

For goods in large bulk it was, in another sense too, a more economic method of transport than road conveyance. The canal barge was a bigger unit than anything on the road. Thirty tons was the average capacity of a 'narrow boat', and many of the craft used on canals were larger—the Humber keel, for example, taking a cargo of 80–100 tons. But here also the advantage was accompanied by a drawback: there was no uniformity of gauge between the canals. Speaking roughly, the canals of the Midlands were 'narrow' (taking craft less than 7 ft. wide), those of the North, of South Wales, and of southern England were 'wide'. Partly for this reason there was little interchange of craft between canals. Indeed, there was little interchange of any kind between the canal companies. They squabbled over their shares of tolls and seldom combined for action in their common interest. Even when they were clearly on the defensive in the nineteenth century they never managed to set up the simplest kind of clearing-house, as the railways did, though they were specifically enjoined to do so by Parliament in 1888.

*　　*　　*

The canals were always primarily concerned with goods traffic. Some of them carried passengers too ⟨103⟩. Passenger boats ran on the Bridgewater Canal for many years from 1769 onwards. The Forth & Clyde was conveying nearly 200,000 passengers a year in 1836; a still brisker trade of the same kind was carried on between Glasgow and Paisley, at a fare of 4*d.* (6*d.* in the cabin) for the eight miles. Among the passenger boats running on the Lancaster Canal was an 'express' put on in 1833, which went from Kendal to Preston in about seven hours. 'I never did enjoy a journey as I did this,' wrote a passenger in 1839. 'It was like a journey in a dream or in an Eastern tale—water, weather, scenery, motion—all were most beautiful.'[51]

But pleasant as such travel might be it could never be rapid, nor in general very convenient. The greatest advances in passenger transport occurred not by water but by land.

The improvement of the roads in the early eighteenth century did not much affect the speed of the regular stage coaches running on them. Four days was the advertised time of the journey from London to York in 1706; it was four days still in 1754. The third quarter of the century, however,

37

brought an improvement, owing in the main to the work of the turnpike trusts. It is true that they were inexpert and often lethargic: yet the cumulative effect of the work they carried through was considerable. It might not at once reduce the time taken by stage coaches. For each trust was concerned with only a short section of road, and the full improvement could not appear until the road had been turnpiked in long stretches. That was a slow process. Though the first experiments in turnpiking began on the Great North Road in 1663, the whole road was not turnpiked throughout to York, Berwick, and Carlisle until 1776.[52] Even then its surface varied according to the energy of successive trustees and their surveyors and according to the geology of the country the road traversed.

Among the early surveyors using empirical methods of making and reconstructing roads, the most remarkable was John Metcalf of Knaresborough: remarkable as one of the first men who can be described as a professional road engineer, more remarkable still in that he was blind. Between 1765 and 1792 he was responsible for the construction of about 180 miles of turnpike road, mainly in Yorkshire. He paid particular attention to the bed of the road and to its drainage, often laying bundles of heather in the foundations, to be covered by stone and gravel. Other surveyors too, their names now almost forgotten, had their own contributions to make. On the Market Harborough–Loughborough road granite setts from Mountsorrel were used for paving in towns from 1787 onwards, and two surveyors named Buswell and Bown were putting down granite chippings shortly afterwards, anticipating in some measure the famous surfacings of Telford and McAdam.[53]

Such improvements had their counterpart in the design of carriages and coaches. Until the middle of the eighteenth century the only springing had been afforded by suspending the body from the framework on stout leather straps ⟨38–9⟩. Now, however, the steel spring made its appearance, at first on private vehicles but soon on stage coaches. In 1754 a service was announced between Edinburgh and London, taking ten days in summer and twelve in winter, by a 'new genteel two-end glass machine [i.e. a coach with glass windows], hung on steel springs, exceeding light and easy'.[54] Such epithets are relative; but this technical development made it possible for the cumbrous stage-coach to move faster.

So great an improvement had been effected by the 1780s, through these and other means, that the stage coach on main roads was outrunning the horse-post. A letter sent by post from Bath took 40 hours to be delivered in London; if it was despatched (illegally) by coach, it could arrive in 17. Naturally, therefore, much revenue was being lost to the Post Office.

A remedy was proposed by John Palmer in 1782: the establishment of special services of coaches for the conveyance of mails. They were to travel at high speed; to convey a small, strictly limited, number of passengers; to be exempt, as the post-boys had always been, from turnpike tolls; and to carry an armed guard. The last proposal was not the least important, for highwaymen had been a curse to travellers, and especially to coach passengers, for a century past ⟨47⟩. Palmer's plan met with some opposition and a good deal of derision from postal officials; but Pitt accepted it, and the first mail coaches began to run between Bristol and London on 2 August 1784. The experiment was an immediate success, and before the end of 1786 mail coaches were running on all the chief roads out of London —to Exeter, Milford Haven, Holyhead, and Edinburgh—as well as on some of the cross roads. Palmer was a cantankerous character. He soon fell out with the Post Office and devoted much energy to the pursuit of claims for compensation: in the end with success, for he enjoyed a pension of £3,000 a year from 1793 onwards and received the sum of £50,000 in addition 20 years later. If he had little of Ralph Allen's patience and none of his sweet nature, Palmer was unquestionably a public benefactor, as more than a dozen towns testified by presenting him with their freedom, from Gloucester to Inverness ⟨73⟩.

The average speed of the first mail coaches was eight miles an hour, including stops; they kept exact time, as the Post Office required; and they ran safely, with no marked increase in accidents in spite of their speed, and free from robbery. Not a single mail coach was held up between 1784 and 1792. Though valuable freight on an ordinary coach or slow stage waggon might still need to be guarded, the trade of the highwayman was dead.

Nevertheless the new coaches, and the increased speeds of the old ones, which had to try to rival them, presented a serious problem to the turnpike trusts: for they demanded ever higher standards of road engineering and maintenance, and the Post Office exercised constant pressure to secure them. A major political interest reinforced that pressure where one road was concerned. The Irish Union of 1801 much increased the traffic across the St. George's Channel, since the Dublin Parliament was now abolished and Irish representatives sat at Westminster. Most of this traffic passed by way of Holyhead, but the Welsh part of the road was vile. A mail coach was put on between Holyhead and Shrewsbury in 1808 and then the service was abandoned because it proved impossible to maintain it with regularity. Two years later an investigation was begun into the cost of making the road perfect for coach traffic.

The survey was entrusted to Thomas Telford, who had begun his career as County Surveyor of Shropshire ⟨95⟩, had gone on to build the Ellesmere Canal with its superb aqueducts ⟨87–9⟩, and was already working for the Government on the Caledonian Canal and on roads and bridges in the Highlands ⟨97⟩. Telford's survey put forward a coherent scheme for the making of a great road between London and Holyhead, worthy to form a central artery of the new United Kingdom. It was not immediately implemented by a Government closely preoccupied with the struggle against Napoleon; but in 1815 a Board of Parliamentary Commissioners was appointed, and under their authority Telford carried out his plans. Though the Board was not intended to supersede the turnpike trusts, seven Welsh trusts were consolidated in 1819 and placed under its management. First and last the great operation involved the planning of a wholly new road 22 miles long from Holyhead across Anglesey and of the Menai Bridge, an astonishing exhibition of the lightness and grace that could be achieved by the suspension principle and the use of iron as a material ⟨96⟩; a reconstruction, so extensive as to amount nearly to new building, of the road through the mountains by Bettws-y-Coed ⟨99⟩ and Corwen to Shrewsbury; and a series of improvements, again adding up almost to reconstruction, of the road on to London through Birmingham and Daventry—the last 70 miles of it, from Weedon, running over the Roman Watling Street. The whole work took over 10 years to complete and cost something like £750,000.

Telford's Holyhead road was new in two senses: in much of its alignment, straighter and far better graded than before he took it in hand; and in its surface, which helped to make travelling smoother and easier than it had ever been in this country before. His methods in building a new first-class road, or reconstructing an old one, were elaborate, requiring a carefully constructed foundation, sound drainage, and an elliptical surface of gravel or stones broken small.

These methods produced the perfection of coach travelling. But they were expensive, and beyond the means of the turnpike trusts. The trustees' oracle came to be not Telford but J. L. McAdam ⟨85⟩, whose hobby had been road-making long before he became General Surveyor to the Bristol Turnpike Trust in 1816. This was a large undertaking, which had consolidated under one control nearly 150 miles of roads, and it gave McAdam an ideal opportunity of putting his ideas into practice. His method of road-making was cheaper than Telford's—it did not, for example, demand any specially-prepared foundation; and his critics were apt to deride it as shoddy. In general, however, the result was excellent, and his authority quickly came to be nationally established. By 1823 he had himself advised 32 turnpike trusts, and his three sons were assisting 85 more. The value of his work lay not only in his system of road-making. His own experience, and that of Telford on the Holyhead road, had shown clearly how desirable it was to amalgamate the small turnpike trusts into strong units of administration. In 1825 he was largely responsible for persuading Parliament to consolidate all the trusts in the neighbourhood of London into one, the

Metropolis Turnpike Trust, which controlled the whole complex system from 1827 to 1872. Towards the end of his life he advocated a measure of direct administration of turnpikes by the State closely similar to the control exercised by the Ministry of Transport today.[55]

Telford and McAdam then, and the large body of men who worked with them and under their influence, gave Britain a system of first-class roads, able to carry coaching services that were the wonder of visitors and took horse-drawn transport to its highest pitch of perfection. The best coaches made an average speed, including stops, of 10 or 11 miles an hour in normal service. In a light post-chaise the proprietor of *The Sun* was able to carry copies of his paper from London to Glasgow, with news of the passing of the Reform Bill through the Lords in 1832, in just under 36 hours, or at an overall speed of $11\frac{1}{4}$ miles an hour.

That dazzling performance owed much, once again, to Telford. Nothing like it would have been possible but for his reconstruction of the road from Carlisle to Glasgow from 1816 onwards. His services to his native country were of peculiar importance, especially perhaps his work under the Commissioners of Roads and Bridges in the Highlands; for with little exaggeration they can be said to take the main pattern of their modern communications from him, saving only those which were to be added by the sparse railway system and a few additions of the twentieth century. True, he was preceded by General Wade: but the roads and bridges Wade built ⟨53⟩ had had a military purpose. Telford was a man of peace, his work designed not to subjugate the Highlands but to improve the social life and the economy of their people. If we take account also of his harbours on the eastern coast from Wick (1808) to Dundee (1814) and of his great canal, which failed through no fault of his own, we can see how great a debt northern Scotland owes to this man from the Border.

As an engineer he enjoyed a national standing: not through political influence or mere personal charm, but through his massive achievement. It was fitting that he should have been the first President of the Institution of Civil Engineers, whose founding in 1818 signalised the emergence of a new profession. Lane's portrait of him, painted for the Institution ⟨86⟩, reflects his serene power. In the background of it, symbolising the whole of his work, we catch sight of the great aqueduct of Pontcysyllte.

The Age of Steam

IN 1830 THE TURNPIKE ROADS of Britain reached the zenith of their efficiency and fame. Thirty years later they were an out-of-date survival, useful still in remote country like mid-Wales and north-west Scotland but superseded as main arteries of communication by the railways. No other change in the history of transport has been at once so rapid and so complete. If any technical development could ever be called a revolution, it was this one.

What made it so astonishing was the swift emergence of the locomotive. There was nothing new about railways. They had existed in this country since early in the seventeenth century, when they were developed almost simultaneously on Tyneside, in Shropshire, and in Nottinghamshire, most commonly as a device for easing the passage of wheeled cart-loads of coal from the pits to navigable water. Their use spread rapidly in the coalfields —and especially in north-eastern England, so that railways came to be known as 'Newcastle roads' in the eighteenth century. The rails were of timber ⟨120⟩, strengthened sometimes with plates of iron but not made wholly of metal until the second half of the century, when iron rails began to be cast at Coalbrookdale and elsewhere. The waggons were moved by horses, by men, or by the force of gravity, not by machines.

The earliest locomotives, or movable steam vehicles, were conceived as running on roads. It was not until 1802 that a locomotive was designed for a railway. The pioneer effort was made at Coalbrookdale; but unhappily we know next to nothing about it. Two years later, however, Richard Trevithick built a locomotive for the Penydarren Ironworks near Merthyr Tydfil that hauled ten tons of iron for nine miles on a railway.

Here was a natural extension of the work that had already been done to develop the stationary steam engine. In the account of its first journey it was observed that 'the number of horses in the kingdom will be very considerably reduced, and the machine, in the hands of the present proprietors, will be made use of in a thousand instances never yet thought of for an engine'. Though the statement was not precisely true of this locomotive, which had a short life, it was a prophetic view of the future of locomotives in general.

Trevithick was a restless genius, and the locomotive was soon displaced in his mind by other schemes, which took him to South America and eventually to a pauper's grave at Dartford. Other people soon adopted the idea. John Blenkinsop, superintendent of a colliery near Leeds, first

42

developed the locomotive as a machine for hauling coal. Following in Trevithick's footsteps, William Hedley of Wylam, Northumberland, demonstrated that the locomotive could perform that work satisfactorily by the mere force of adhesion on smooth rails, without the aid of a rack ⟨136⟩. The men who did most for the locomotive, however, were unquestionably George and Robert Stephenson.

George Stephenson did not invent the locomotive; in so far as that achievement is to be ascribed to any single man, the credit for it belongs to Trevithick. But by his experimental work and by his personal advocacy he succeeded in establishing the locomotive as an instrument capable of much more than the haulage of coal over short distances. In 1821 he persuaded Edward Pease ⟨124⟩ and his fellow-directors of the Stockton & Darlington Railway that their line should be laid out on the assumption that the new machines would be used; and locomotives performed most of the haulage on the railway from its opening in 1825 ⟨125⟩. In collaboration with his son Robert—an engineer as able as himself—George Stephenson then tackled the much more formidable operation of building the Liverpool & Manchester Railway (1826–30).

The demand for this railway sprang directly from the deficiencies and mismanagement of the previously established means of transport; and the key to its success was the locomotive. The whole future of railways was staked on this great undertaking. If the Liverpool & Manchester had failed, that might well have meant that the railway would be confined to the slow haulage of heavy freight. It was the Stephensons' triumph to show that, by the use of locomotives, speeds far in excess of those of the fastest coach could easily be attained in ordinary service. From the day of its opening on 15 September 1830, the number of coaches travelling between the two towns decreased; within two years only one was left, such was the speed of the locomotive and its general reliability in service. Since the Liverpool & Manchester Railway carried both passengers and freight, the full potentialities of the new mode of transport were demonstrated at once ⟨126⟩.

The railway as we know it emerges quite clearly in 1830. After a short initial period of uncertainty, its triumph was rapid and decisive. People watched the Liverpool & Manchester line with the closest interest, both in this country and abroad, and they scrutinised the financial results of its working. What they saw impressed them deeply. Though the usual delays, inevitable in the operation of such a complex machine as a railway, occurred from time to time, they were not more numerous or more troublesome than those to which the coaches had always been liable. On the whole the system worked smoothly. The company was able to pay an average dividend of nearly 10 per cent over the first decade of its working.

In the light of these results, and the hardly less successful operation of other early lines like the Stockton & Darlington and the Newcastle & Carlisle, schemes for extending railways in all parts of the country were quickly formed. There was a boom in railway projection in 1836–37, which produced, it is true, a number of unsuccessful companies but also the skeleton of a national railway system: the lines built under powers obtained in these years stretched from London to Brighton, Exeter, Liverpool, Leeds, and Colchester, besides the most important internal line in Scotland, that connecting Edinburgh and Glasgow. While these railways were still being built, a further intense speculation set in during the years 1845–48: the 'Railway Mania', as it was called at the time and has been called ever since. This was speculation on the largest scale, resulting in the projection of hundreds of futile and fraudulent companies, which engulfed, without return, the money of those who invested in them. But the Mania had constructive results. By the time it was over, and the railway-building arising from it was complete, about 1852, almost the whole of the main lines of the English system, as we know them now, had been laid down. Only the remoter parts of Britain still waited to be reached by the railway. Wilkie Collins could write a book about Cornwall entitled *Rambles beyond Railways* in 1851—though only eight years were to pass before Cornwall was linked to the rest of England by Brunel's Royal Albert Bridge at Saltash. The main lines nosed their way along the coasts of Wales to New Milford and Holyhead, but the interior knew little of them until the sixties ⟨182⟩. In Scotland, though Aberdeen could be reached from the south by 1850, the railway did not strike out north and west into the Highlands until 1856–80. Nevertheless, it is true to say that the greater part of the British railway system was constructed in little more than 20 years, between 1830 and 1852.

The railway effected a very striking improvement in communications. 'Everything is near, everything is immediate,' wrote Sydney Smith in 1842, 'time, distance, and delay are abolished.'[56] Yet it should be remembered that the coaches had gone a long way towards abolishing time and distance during the previous hundred years. It had taken $4\frac{1}{2}$ days to get from London to Manchester in 1754; by 1837 this time had been reduced to 18 hours. The further reduction to 12 hours on the opening of the railway in 1838, even if it undoubtedly represented a welcome improvement, was only carrying an established process further. Though the first express trains in the world, travelling at really high speeds, ran between Paddington and Exeter in 1848, they were not imitated at the time and were slowed up in pursuit of economy in 1852. The heyday of the express train did not begin until the eighties.

The speed of the railway was its most spectacular characteristic, but it was not the only important one. Two other services that it rendered to its passengers counted for as much. In the first place, it was notably cheaper to travel by train than it had been by coach. This does not always appear at first sight, for the quoted fares for comparable accommodation some-times show very little difference. Comparing the price of 'inside' places in a stage coach of the 1830s with that of first-class tickets on the railway in 1860, a journey from London to Birmingham cost a guinea by coach and a pound by railway; the difference to Liverpool, similarly, was only five shillings. But the real cost of coach travel had always been more than the quoted fare. The guard and coachman had to be tipped at each stage, a serious nuisance that added 20 per cent or more to the price paid for a ticket; and the long journey by coach obliged the traveller to take expen-sive meals at hotels on the road, which the quicker journey by railway reduced or obviated altogether.[57] To the poorer traveller the difference was greater still. After the passing of the Cheap Trains Act of 1844 he could count on a train on every line running at not less than 12 miles an hour—whereas the fastest coach had not exceeded 11—at a fare of a penny a mile, and in accommodation protected from the weather instead of on the dangerous and exposed roof of a coach.

Most important of all, the railway changed the whole scale of human movement. The service provided by the mail coach in the 1820s and 1830s was an impressive achievement, but it was available to no more than a tiny fraction of the whole population. The coach was a very small unit, conveying from a dozen to twenty people. The railway, on the other hand, carried its passengers not by tens but by hundreds. By the fifties, when plant and equipment had been increased in quantity and scale, it was usually possible to run additional trains when they were needed without difficulty. Six million people visited the Great Exhibition in 1851. If they had been dependent upon road transport, the figure could not have reached a tenth of this.

What this means is that the railway gave the ordinary man in England a new freedom to move when and where he liked, both by providing the equipment and by cheapening the cost of transport. It afforded employ-ment on a vast scale, first in the construction of the lines themselves and then in the railway service. It enlarged very greatly the distance at which people could live from their work, moving scores of thousands of people in and out of London and the great cities every day. It made the fortune of the popular seaside resorts with excursion trains ⟨148⟩. It enabled the un-employed or the poorly paid workman to move easily and quickly away from home in search of a better living. And it rendered possible a further extension of the already highly developed postal system of Britain, which made it a wonder for speed and cheapness to the rest of the world.

All this had its counterpart in the movement of freight. If the railway had emerged in the seventeenth and eighteenth centuries largely as a transporter of coal, it moved in the nineteenth century into the business of carrying every conceivable kind of merchandise, heavy and light, large and small, in any quantity the consignor might choose to name. It was the railway that made possible the development of mass-production on a great scale: whether of Accrington bricks or of Penrhyn slates or of Bessemer steel from Sheffield. The railway, too, gradually reached out its tentacles into mid-Wales and the Highlands of Scotland, until it engulfed the cattle trade that had so long gone on the hoof with the drovers ⟨83–4⟩: the last of the great Trysts, or drovers' markets, at Falkirk was held in 1901. Nothing was proof against the railways' power. And just as the canal companies had been attacked by merchants and manufacturers for their high rates in the early years of the nineteenth century, so the railways were freely denounced as 'monopolists', charging rates that were exorbitant, in the seventies and eighties. These accusations were often substantiated. Yet the railways rendered a priceless service to Great Britain. They contributed, as much as any other single factor, to her industrial primacy in the world.

Great Britain, moreover, had become, and remained throughout these years, the chief supplier both of engineering skill and of plant and materials to railways overseas.* British contractors built railways all over the Continent: from Paris to Dieppe, Le Havre and Cherbourg, from Orléans to Bordeaux; from Culoz to Turin (excepting only the Mont Cenis Tunnel, and that Italian achievement owed much to the boring machine of an Englishman, Thomas Bartlett). Later in the century, British capital and British engineers played a leading part in the development of railways in South America.

The first British locomotives crossed the Atlantic to the United States in 1828–29. When the Russian Government wanted a railway engine it turned to Timothy Hackworth of Shildon, Co. Durham; and it was his son John, then aged seventeen, who demonstrated the machine before the Tsar at Tsarskoye-Selo in 1836. All through the thirties and forties Britain furnished locomotives on a large scale to the railways of Europe; and if France, Belgium, and Germany were building most of their own by the fifties, she continued to supply countries like Holland and Spain, which never established great railway workshops. By the sixties her railway machinery was going further afield: to South America, to India and Australasia and China.

Some of the works that supplied all this plant became very large: important elements in the economy of the towns in which they were situated.

* This theme will be illustrated further in a subsequent volume in this series, *Britain and the World*.

And just as Stourport and Goole had grown into towns from insignificant hamlets entirely through water transport, and Birkenhead through shipping, so the 'railway towns' came to form a recognisable group in the economic geography of Great Britain. They varied considerably. Sometimes—as at Darlington, Doncaster, and Derby—the railway settled on an old town and dominated it, for a time at least, completely. One ancient town, Carlisle, though it never had any railway works on a large scale, came to earn its living chiefly as a railway junction: no ordinary junction indeed, for it gathered up the lines of seven separate companies. Several other towns owe their creation and development primarily to railways, the facilities they afforded and the capital they were willing to invest. The Manchester, Sheffield & Lincolnshire Railway provided Cleethorpes with its amenities as a seaside resort—promenade, gardens, even shopping arcade. Barrow-in-Furness, with its astonishing growth from 250 people in 1841 to 47,250 in 1881, was a creature of the Furness Railway, which financed the construction of the docks, provided the town with its early public services such as gas and water, and built the Town and Market Halls. The railway company has been described without exaggeration as 'the *de facto* government of Barrow'.[58]

But there were three railway towns *par excellence*: Swindon, Eastleigh, and Crewe. In a special sense they are the creation of the railway. New Swindon, an addition to an old market town, was developed by the Great Western Railway in consequence of the decision to establish its central works there in 1840. Eastleigh grew up half a century later, in the rural parish of South Stoneham, close to Southampton. Until 1891 the London & South Western Railway built all the vehicles it needed at its Nine Elms Works in South London. The carriage works were then moved to Eastleigh, followed by the locomotive works sixteen years afterwards. Crewe, like Swindon, developed early; not in proximity to an old town, however, but like Eastleigh in a quiet countryside. It was in 1840 that the Grand Junction Railway decided to construct its works in the parish of Coppenhall, a central point on its system that had already been fixed upon as the junction for Chester and Manchester. The town was laid out in accordance with plans prepared by the company's engineer, Joseph Locke, and an architect named John Cunningham. The first houses were occupied in 1842. By 1851 the population was over 4,000, and it grew steadily to ten times that number by the end of the century. A committee of the Grand Junction company was set up in 1842 to superintend the settlement; three years later its function was baldly defined as 'to take charge of . . . the general management of the town of Crewe'. When Christ Church was erected in 1845, the railway company contributed largely towards the cost, and the patronage of the living was vested in four directors. The company built over 800 houses in the town, superior in quality to those of private builders. The railway's social activities extended improbably far. It undertook the scavenging of the streets, established a savings bank, provided allotments, and as early as 1845 opened public baths. This benevolence was always autocratic. F. W. Webb, the London & North Western company's Chief Mechanical Engineer, tried to ensure that the railway's servants voted Conservative; declared Liberals and Radicals were systematically deprived of their jobs. But this victimisation ultimately proved a failure. The town emancipated itself from Tory control, with a resounding Liberal victory, in 1891.[59]

A railway company was something different from any commercial organisation that had preceded it. In the first place it was bigger. In 1899 the capital, revenue, and expenditure of the three largest British companies, the Great Western, London & North Western, and Midland, were as follows:[60]

	Capital created or sanctioned at 31 Dec. 1899			Revenue in 1899	Expenditure in 1899
	Stocks and shares	Loans	Total		
	£	£	£	£	£
GWR	68,221,412	24,060,625	92,282,037	10,806,596	6,424,042
LNWR	81,373,233	39,638,321	121,011,554	13,797,057	10,801,911
MR	137,699,918	36,005,230	173,705,148	11,004,222	8,892,935
Total	287,294,563	99,704,176	386,998,739	35,607,875	26,118,888

These sums were expended on, and received from, a great variety of activities besides those of moving trains on rails. The railway companies were deeply interested in other forms of transport. They owned canals and operated all forms of road haulage, including buses. They were carriers on their own track, as the turnpike trusts had never been on roads and the canal companies seldom were on their own water. They ran ferries and fleets of steamers, for cargo and passengers, plying to Ireland and the Continent ⟨188, 192⟩. Other companies besides the Furness invested heavily in docks: the North Eastern at Middlesbrough and the Hartlepools, the Caledonian at Grangemouth, the London & South Western most spectacularly when it acquired Southampton Docks in 1892 and developed them, with striking success, as a southern rival to Liverpool. The railways built and ran hotels, so that British Railways today own the greatest chain of hotels in Europe. Their industrial activities had wide ramifications. The Great Eastern and the London, Chatham & Dover companies did their own printing; the London & South Western supplied the ballast for the whole of its track from its granite quarry at Meldon, near Okehampton; the Great Western and the London & North Western fuelled their locomotives in part with coal mined in their own pits.

Yet for all the railways' success and the imposing scale of their laby- rinthine operations, they never achieved a monopoly of transport in Britain. In the 1830s and 1840s it looked as if they might. They were momentarily theatened by the competition of steam carriages on the roads ⟨150–1⟩; but those vehicles proved too unreliable, and on occasion too dangerous ⟨152⟩, to win acceptance. Wherever the railway extended, it killed almost instantly the coach services that ran parallel with it. With effortless ease the railways inherited the coaches' business: whether on the great trunk routes ⟨154⟩ or in those districts, like the West Riding of Yorkshire, where the coaches had built up an intensive inter-urban ser- vice.[61] The most prudent and far-seeing coach-owners accommodated themselves to the change adroitly. Messrs. Chaplin & Horne sold out of coaching and transferred their interest to the railways, Chaplin becoming chairman of the London & South Western company in 1843–52 and again in 1854–58. The great freight-carrying firm of Pickford's associated itself with the Liverpool & Manchester, London & Birmingham, and Grand Junction Railways. Smaller men recognised that the best thing they could do was not to oppose the railway but to turn to running feeders to it; and these continued for a time to be modestly profitable. As in the fifties and sixties the railway system was extended, with the multiplication of branch lines, the demand for these feeder services declined. Almost every town of any importance in England and Wales had a railway station: of those that did not perhaps the largest was Shaftesbury. But carriers' services still had their value in linking villages to market-towns and railway stations. They survived even in the neighbourhood of London. Albert Adams issued a card in 1859 announcing that his 'cart or van' would be plying between St. Albans and London twice a week,[62] though one wonders if he continued in business after the opening of the direct Midland Railway line to St. Pancras in 1868. In the seventies and eighties carriers' waggons are still a familiar part of the scene in Hardy's novels: Mrs. Dollery's van, for instance, that opens *The Woodlanders*.

In these circumstances the turnpike trusts naturally suffered: between 1837 and 1850 their collective revenues fell by a third. But their fortunes varied greatly, according to their situation and their financial liabilities. On the road between Liverpool and Manchester the Eccles bar, which had been let at £1,700 in 1830, found no bidders when offered at £800 in 1831; nor would any one give £500 for the Irlam bar which had been let in 1830 at £1,300.[63] An old-established and prosperous trust, like that for the road from Market Harborough to Loughborough, found its revenue much decreased through the withdrawal of the long-distance coach services: yet it kept a large local traffic, and the receipts from tolls remained fairly steady, if at a lower level than in the early thirties, down to 1867. In Dorset the Sherborne Turnpike Trust was able to undertake a very considerable improvement of the road leading out of the town to the south in 1848; and it may well have proved a sound investment, for no railway was ever built in that direction. On the other hand, the Wimborne and Puddletown turnpike was a disastrous venture. It was undertaken in 1841 and lost most of its traffic six years later to the Southampton & Dorchester Railway. When the trust was wound up in 1878 it was calculated that one of its original promoters, Mr. Drax of Charborough Park, had lost £48,000 in principal and interest.[64]

If some trusts remained solvent, even prosperous, others went bankrupt or became so impoverished that they could not maintain their roads. Faced with this problem, Parliament authorised the county magistrates in 1841 to make a contribution from the highway rates to assist the turnpike trusts. This imposition was resented with violence in South Wales. Turnpike riots had not been uncommon in the eighteenth century. These were far more widespread and formidable. The rioting mobs were frequently led by men disguised as women, and they claimed to be 'Rebecca and her children', alluding to the promise made to Isaac's wife in Genesis xxiv. 60 that her seed should 'possess the gate of those which hate them'.[65] With systematic efficiency these bands set themselves to destroy the turnpike gates. In the counties of Pembroke and Cardigan not one was left; 80 were demolished in Carmarthenshire. The Government yielded. In 1844 it abolished the trusts throughout the six counties of South Wales, compensating their creditors and transferring their work to County Roads Boards. The Boards then greatly reduced the tolls levied, thus removing the popular grievance, and at the same time they so improved the administration that within thirty years they were virtually clear of all debt. It is a pity that there were no Rebecca riots elsewhere in Britain, leading to the same admirable expedient. As it was, the turnpike trusts were wound up very gradually. The last toll was levied, on the Anglesey section of the Holyhead road, on 1 November 1895.[66]

Meanwhile, under the Local Government Act of 1888, the new County Councils had become, for all practical purposes, road authorities, superseding at last the parishes on whom the burden of maintenance had first been placed statutorily in 1555. The change came about without attracting much comment; but we can now see how timely it was, enabling roads to be better administered, in long continuous units, on the eve of an unexpected revival of their use.

Such was the impact of railways upon road transport. What of their effect on inland waterways and coastal shipping?

The steam-operated railway represented as clear a threat to the canals as to the proprietors of coaches and the turnpike trusts. Many of the early railways were promoted quite frankly in order to break the hold of canal companies—just as some canals, like the Sankey Navigation, had been promoted to break the turnpikes' monopoly. In his admirably cogent *Letter on the Subject of the Projected Rail Road between Liverpool and Manchester* (1824), Joseph Sandars had no difficulty in showing that the Bridgewater Canal Trustees and the proprietors of the Mersey & Irwell Navigation and the Rochdale Canal were all extorting charges substantially higher than those authorised by Parliament, which were being paid because there was no convenient alternative means of transport. The profits made from these waterways were notoriously large: the 39 original shareholders in the Mersey & Irwell Navigation, for example, had been paid an average dividend of 50 per cent for nearly 50 years. Nothing but fierce new competition, it was plain, would break such a monopoly; and that was what the railway, most formidably, provided.

Not all canal proprietors were so grasping and short-sighted. Some were criticised not for their extortionate charges but for the inadequate services they afforded. This was the ground of complaint against the Glamorganshire Canal, the most important of the Welsh waterways. It ran from Merthyr Tydfil to Cardiff and at Abercynon it received, by means of the Penydarren Tramroad, the iron export from Dowlais and its neighbourhood. In the 1830s this was rapidly growing—it increased by 50 per cent in 1835–39; and the canal became intolerably congested, even though traffic passed along it by night as well as by day, the locks being lit by gas or oil. There were further delays, too, in loading the sea-going ships at Cardiff. The canal company, it seemed, could do no more; and the ironmasters and coal-owners decided to promote a railway between the same points, running along the same valley. They succeeded. The Taff Vale Railway was authorised in 1836 and opened in 1840–41. It did not ruin the canal, which continued to pay a dividend of 8 per cent down to 1876. But the railway did much better, until in the eighties—with an irony frequent enough in transport history—it was overtaken by exactly the same criticism that the canal had faced in the thirties. The railway and the docks at Cardiff and Penarth could not get the coal away fast enough, and the Barry Dock & Railways company was formed, against the bitterest opposition of the Taff Vale, in 1884.[67]

The truth was that, for most purposes, the railway could offer better facilities than the canal, at a more economic rate. The units it could handle were almost infinitely flexible, from a single parcel to a 500-ton train of coal; the speed of the railway was greater, and in the eighties and nineties it became greater still; the network of railways, as it grew in the Victorian age, was far more extensive than that of the waterways had ever been. It was a simpler matter to build sidings or a branch line from an existing railway to a factory than to cut a new waterway. In the second half of the nineteenth century most new industrial development was sited along railway lines rather than canals.

Many canals, however, refused to succumb quietly to railway competition, fighting fiercely to retain their traffic, sometimes with a fair measure of success. The Weaver and the Aire & Calder Navigations remained independent and prosperous. In 1868 the Oxford Canal was carrying 7 per cent more traffic than it had carried in 1828. But then it is to be noted that its receipts for these services had fallen by about 75 per cent—a striking illustration of the general reduction of freight charges that railway competition brought.[68] The general practice was for the railways to buy out the canals. In the three years 1845–47 they acquired nearly 1,000 miles of waterways, including such great units as the Trent & Mersey, the Shropshire Union, and the Birmingham Canals. Some of the small waterways became derelict in consequence. The railways have been charged, from that time to this, with 'strangling' the canals, as a matter of deliberate policy. The accusation is frequently just; but it is a mistake to discuss the process in emotional or moral terms, as if there were something inherently wicked in it. There was not. It represented the victory of a stronger economic instrument over a weaker one; of a more flexible technique, whose potentialities were still being expanded, over one that had shown its capabilities and was now old-fashioned and on the defensive. Moreover, the railways did not kill, without discrimination, all the canals they took over. The Birmingham Canal Navigations were acquired by the London & North Western Railway, under which, says the canals' modern historian, they were 'well maintained and improved'.[69] By the terms of the take-over the railway guaranteed the canal proprietors a dividend of 4 per cent, and from 1874 onwards it was obliged to supplement the canal company's receipts to the amount necessary to pay the dividend every year. In other words, railway control substantially increased the value of this canal as an investment.

A few of the canals offered a gallant resistance to their rivals. The Lancaster Canal took a lease of the Lancaster & Preston Railway in 1842 and might well have kept the railway under its control if it had not become an important link in the West Coast route to Scotland, so valuable that the Lancaster & Carlisle Railway was willing to buy the lessees out on handsome terms. The Staffordshire & Worcestershire Canal maintained a spirited opposition to railways, and alone among the great companies tried to secure joint action—between the canals in the Birmingham district, for instance—to oppose railway Bills during the Mania in 1845. The attempt failed; but the Staffordshire & Worcestershire never lost heart, and later in the century it did much to prevent the navigation of the Severn from falling into the hands of the railways.

Such steady resistance by a canal company to the railways was rare. The railways had little difficulty in establishing their ascendancy. Towards the close of the nineteenth century the decline and extinction of so many canals began to cause serious disquiet. The railways were by now under fire as monopolists, much as the canals had been in the 1820s and 1830s, and it was natural to argue that the canals ought to be revived to compete with them. From 1873 onwards legislation was passed with a view to restricting the power of the railways over the canals they controlled. In 1882 a movement began for constructing a ship canal from Manchester to the sea: inspired partly, it is true, by the alleged extortion of the port authorities at Liverpool, but more generally by the rates demanded for the carriage of goods on the railways and on the Bridgewater Navigation, which had passed virtually under railway control ten years earlier. Against fierce opposition the Manchester Ship Canal was authorised in 1885 ⟨200–1⟩. It was opened in 1894, at the formidable cost of £14 million, and after a shaky start it grew steadily more prosperous. It was the greatest waterway ever constructed in Britain. Its minimum depth was 28 ft., allowing ships of 12,500 tons to pass up to Manchester. The Canal thus created a new inland port, which has now come to take third position among the ports of the whole country.

If the Manchester Ship Canal was in the end a triumphant success, justifying the hopes of its backers, it has remained unique. Birmingham traders complained likewise of the railways' rates in the eighties, and likewise demanded a ship canal to the sea. But they are still as far as ever from achieving that objective. Nor has any progress been made with plans for a ship canal across the 'waist' of Scotland.

One important explanation of the decline of the canals is that they adopted mechanical haulage so late. William Symington tried out a paddle steamer on the Forth & Clyde Navigation in 1789 and another, the *Charlotte Dundas*, in 1802, whose performance was so successful that the Duke of Bridgewater ordered eight more vessels of the same design for his own canal. The Forth & Clyde proprietors were made nervous by the damage caused to the banks from the wash of the paddles; the Duke died in 1803 and his order was never fulfilled. Twenty years later the investigation was reopened. In 1826 a paddle steamer made its way from Birmingham to London with a cargo of 20 tons, and in the same year a steam tug began working in the Islington tunnel of the Regent's Canal. In 1829–30 the Forth & Clyde company again experimented with steamboats, with somewhat better success than before. Very gradually tugs made their way on to the larger canals. Yet even in 1864 they were restricted in their working over the navigable part of the Severn, and it was not until the seventies that they began to supersede horses on the narrow canals.

There were some good reasons for the caution of the waterways over adopting steam haulage. The original problem that had deterred the Forth & Clyde company was never completely solved; the gain in speed was less striking than might be expected; in a steamboat (as distinct from a tug) much valuable cargo space had to be sacrificed to the machinery, and it must always be remembered that the size of canal boats was strictly limited by the length and breadth of the locks they had to negotiate. Yet, even in the face of these objections, mechanical haulage did become general by the end of the century. If the canals had been more enterprising they would have adopted steam power 50 years earlier.

This tardiness stands in strong contrast to the speed and enthusiasm with which steam propulsion was introduced on the railways and on their great competitor, coastal shipping. Ten years after Symington's experiments with the *Charlotte Dundas* Henry Bell placed the *Comet* in service on the Clyde between Glasgow, Greenock, and Helensburgh. She was the first commercially successful steamboat in Europe—though not in the world, for steamship services were already in operation in the United States. The success of the *Comet* was immediate, and steamboats soon became a familiar sight on the Clyde ⟨116⟩, which may claim to be the cradle of European steam navigation. The *Comet* herself ended her days by running ashore on Craignish Point in 1820, on the regular service she had established in the previous year between Glasgow and Fort William. It is one more sign of the constant attempts being made in the early nineteenth century to bring the Hebrides and the Highlands into closer touch with the rest of Scotland that this pioneer steamer should have been used so early for that service.

Elsewhere in Britain the steamer quickly established itself in the coasting trade, as a carrier both of freight and of passengers. Even when railways were completed between Aberdeen, Edinburgh, and London many passengers travelled by sea: some because they preferred sea travel for its own sake, more because the fares remained very low. The steamer also built up a wholly new passenger trade in conveying passengers for pleasure trips along the coasts, from Margate and Brighton and Weymouth, in the Bristol Channel ⟨189⟩ and the Firth of Clyde ⟨190⟩. By the middle of the nineteenth century the steamer was in command on all the cross-Channel services, which were run to an increasing extent in collaboration with the railways. These services imposed exacting conditions, in endurance, speed, and amenities, and the challenges they presented brought about important improvements in naval architecture ⟨191⟩.

The steamship thus became ubiquitous and indispensable: whether as a liner for crossing the Atlantic or as a water-bus for carrying passengers on the crowded Thames or Clyde ⟨192⟩.

Internal Combustion

THE RAILWAYS ESTABLISHED a preponderant power in British transport, though never a monopoly, in the middle of the nineteenth century. They retained it down to the first World War. But even before 1914 they had to face one formidable challenge, and to admit a measure of defeat; whilst a second, more formidable still, was showing well above the horizon.

When the railways were new they did little to stimulate suburban traffic. Their role was that of trunk routes; their chief rivals the stage coach and the canal. It was a long time before the great companies realised the potential profit this traffic might bring them. When the London & Birmingham Railway was opened from Euston to Boxmoor in 1837, its first station was at Harrow, 11½ miles out. Although others were added at Willesden, Sudbury, and Pinner six years later, in 1845 the local service was limited to three down and five up trains on week-days, only one of which conveyed third-class passengers.[70] Other railways—the Greenwich and Blackwall companies in London, a few in the provinces like the Newcastle & North Shields—had by then begun to exploit suburban traffic; but they were small concerns, for which that task was vital from the outset. It was companies like these, and others which had no great long-distance traffic in passengers or freight, such as the Great Eastern and the London, Brighton & South Coast, that did most for suburban development. The great main-line companies regarded a heavy suburban traffic quite frankly as a nuisance, blocking the passage of their expresses and coal trains. C. H. Grinling, writing *The History of the Great Northern Railway* at the end of the nineteenth century, repeatedly refers to 'the suburban incubus' that the company bore in respect of its lines from King's Cross to Edgware, Barnet, Hitchin, and Enfield. It has been

E

well observed that of the five Home Counties, Middlesex, which depended most for its railway services on the main-line companies, was the least developed in the Victorian age.[71]

The railway played very little part at first in moving passengers within London itself. A Royal Commission on Metropolitan Termini recommended in 1846 that, as far as possible, railways should be altogether prohibited from entering inner London; it made a few exceptions, however, one of them in favour of a line extending on an embankment along the north shore of the Thames. This recommendation was largely followed, though in the sixties and seventies four railways were permitted to cross the river from the south, on four remarkably ugly bridges, and the North London and Great Eastern companies entered the City, with adjacent termini on Liverpool Street.

All these lines carried a steadily increasing number of suburban passengers into London and out of it every morning and evening. But when they arrived at their terminus they had either to walk or to take horse transport. The omnibus had been introduced into London (under inspiration from Paris) by George Shillibeer in 1829, and it had caught on at once —to become an accepted institution in *Sketches by Boz*, published in 1836. For a brief spell in the 1830s it looked as if buses might become mechanised, with the appearance of the steam carriages built by Walter Hancock of Stratford ⟨151⟩. Three of them plied between Paddington and the City with some success; but they were heavy on the roads, and the turnpike trusts managed to kill them, leaving the horse-buses to dispute for the traffic with cabs (including the new hansoms, which were lighter and faster, taking two people only) and water transport. By 1850 there were some 3,000 buses on the London streets, charging fares at flat rates of 3d. and 6d. Some of the routes were long: from St. John's Wood to Camberwell, for example, from London Bridge to Kensington.[72]

The congestion caused by the multiplication of these and other horse-drawn vehicles now frequently brought traffic to a standstill; and in 1853 a company secured powers to drive a railway underground from Paddington to Farringdon Street. Its line, less than four miles long, was among the most expensive yet built—the cost on some sections working out as high as £100 a yard—and it took ten years to complete. The opening of this Metropolitan Railway on 10 January 1863 is an important event; for it was the first urban underground railway in the world.

Within the next 25 years similar railways multiplied. The 'Inner Circle' was completed (unhappily under the control of two companies, which squabbled incessantly) in 1884; and by that time the system had extended westwards to Hammersmith and Addison Road, northwards to Harrow, eastwards to Whitechapel and New Cross. The western lines did not run underground; but the East London line passed below the river through Sir Marc Brunel's Thames Tunnel of 1825–43 ⟨157⟩.

The Metropolitan Railway did good service in another respect too: by providing a junction with some of the main lines and so enabling their trains to run through to the City. It also provided the sole north–south link between the great trunk lines out of King's Cross and St. Pancras and the London, Chatham & Dover Railway south of the Thames.

The early underground railways had two serious drawbacks, nevertheless. Their construction, in tunnels only a few feet below ground level, was costly and caused the utmost inconvenience through the disturbance of streets and demolition of property; and the sulphurous atmosphere produced by the steam engines made the trains disagreeable to travel in. After a number of earlier experiments, a solution was found to both these problems when the City & South London Railway was opened, from King William Street under the river to Stockwell, in 1890. This ran entirely in 'tube' tunnels, over 40 ft. below the ground, and it was worked by electric locomotives. Its success was clear. No more of the shallow underground lines were built in London (though Paris adopted them from 1900 onwards). The 'tube' system developed fast. Within 20 years it extended to Shepherd's Bush, Hampstead, Finsbury Park, and Clapham ⟨203–4⟩.

London was not the only British city with formidable traffic problems in its streets. But only two of the others adopted expedients as costly and drastic to meet them. Liverpool tried a solution much favoured in the United States: an Overhead Railway carried above the streets on viaducts and an iron framework. It was opened in 1893–96 and operated electrically, with automatic signalling. A Subway was built at Glasgow, running on a circular route under the city in tube tunnels and operated by cable haulage, in 1896. Elsewhere—in Birmingham and Manchester and Edinburgh— nothing but surface transport was provided.

Horse tramways had been introduced into this country by an American in 1860 ⟨169⟩ and regulated by a general Tramways Act ten years later. Together with horse buses they could sometimes provide an intensive service, and they often ran far out into the country. At Leeds, for example, horse trams were running from the centre of the town to Kirkstall and Hunslet every ten minutes throughout the day in 1879; and the bus services extended northwards as far as Adel and Scarcroft, each some five miles out.[73]

Such services as these had less effect on urban development than might perhaps be supposed. They were of importance chiefly to the middle and lower-middle class, in enabling them to live further from their work. The fares charged were usually high: too high for men of the working class to incur as part of the expenses of their daily life. Nevertheless, as building land near the centres of great towns grew steadily more valuable, and as it was eroded by street developments and railway extensions, it became more and more difficult for working men to live in decency near their work. A partial solution to both these problems was afforded by the institution of workmen's fares on the railways in the sixties, which allowed working men to travel by specified trains in the early morning and evening at a fare of one or two shillings a week. By the early eighties some seven million such journeys a year were being made in London; and the requirement to run workmen's trains was made general by the Cheap Trains Act of 1883. One railway company went wholeheartedly into the business: the Great Eastern, which offered a twopenny return fare over distances running up to $10\frac{3}{4}$ miles each way. A London County Council report of 1892 described it as 'especially the workmen's London railway'.

But by the end of the century the Great Eastern found itself unable to transport satisfactorily the whole of the great suburban traffic it had created. The opening of the Central London Railway in 1900 encouraged plans for an extension of tube railways to Leyton and Walthamstow. If they did not in fact materialise for 30 years, another threat was coming immediately: that provided by the electric tram.

*   *   *

Under the Act of 1870 tramways had developed apace ⟨170–1⟩. Until 1877 all motive power was provided by horses; but in that year, after a number of experiments, a regular service of steam trams began to be provided by the Vale of Clyde Tramways at Govan. Two years later statutory conditions were laid down for the use of mechanical traction on tramways. They were stringent. All locomotives were to be kept below a top speed of 10 m.p.h., their working parts were to be concealed, they were not to discharge smoke, steam, or water. Operating within these limitations, the steam tram was of restricted use. But it enabled larger units to be moved than horses could tackle: some cars carried as many as 100 passengers.

Another system of mechanical haulage, free from some of the disabling restrictions imposed on steam traction, was by cable. It was first demonstrated in this country on Highgate Hill in 1884 and appeared in Edinburgh five years later. There it proved successful, solving the problem of moving trams in from the northern suburbs, running up slopes too steep for horses. Between 1890 and 1908 it was steadily extended through all parts of the city and its inner suburbs. Yet its working involved grave mechanical difficulties, some of which were never entirely conquered; and Edinburgh remained unique among British towns in adopting cable working for its tramway system as a whole.[74]

Neither steam nor cable traction was a wholly successful expedient for mechanising tramways. But the problem was evidently urgent as the great towns grew relentlessly in size and the demands on their horse transport became harder and harder to meet. Another solution was now beginning to be worked out: the use of electric power. Short stretches of electric railway were brought into operation at Brighton, Blackpool, and Ryde in 1884–85. Electric trams were introduced into Leeds in 1891; and in 1893–94 they appeared in Staffordshire, Guernsey, and the Isle of Man. Towards the end of the century electric traction spread rapidly. By 1901 great cities like Glasgow and Liverpool had changed over to it; the entire tramway system of Cardiff was converted in the year 1902.

These changes meant major operations for the towns in which they occurred. Physically, in the provision of new fixed equipment ⟨208⟩; and economically because they often involved the purchase of the tramways by the municipality. The first Corporation to operate its own tramways was Huddersfield, which secured powers for this purpose in 1882 because no private company would undertake the task. At first very few other Corporations followed suit: the business was troublesome, and not profitable enough to justify itself. But in the nineties a new factor appeared. The value of electric power, for lighting and other purposes, was clearly demonstrated; and municipalities, following the lead given by Bradford in 1889, began to establish power stations of their own, to provide electricity at once for transport and for all other public services. Manchester decided in principle to do this in 1895, and after prolonged bargaining with its Tramways Company completed the conversion of the old privately-owned system in 1903.

The superiority of electric to horse-drawn trams, from the passenger's point of view, was not open to dispute, and in most substantial towns the change-over was quickly effected. The passing of the horse-drawn vehicle was a matter for sentimental regrets, no more; it lingered on only in such citadels of reaction as Oxford and Cambridge. One objection that was raised against the new system was, however, serious. Unless the current was transmitted to the car from underneath the ground—a costly expedient—it had to be supplied from overhead wires that were unsightly in themselves and involved cluttering up the streets with the poles from which they were suspended. In some places they were forbidden on these grounds. In the early years of the century, following behind developments in the provinces, the London tramway system grew fast; but the L.C.C. moved less rapidly than the private companies, largely because it had to adopt underground transmission—to avoid, for example, destroying the amenities of the Embankment, the most spectacular new street to be cut in Victorian London. In the same way Eastbourne, a seaside resort under aristocratic control, very conscious of the value of preserving its elegant character, declined to have trams at all. In 1903 it went straight over to their new and comparatively untried rival: the motor bus.

*   *   *

The early development of the internal combustion engine for use in transport was a slow and hesitant business. The steam carriages of the 1830s having been driven off the roads, no more mechanically-propelled vehicles were put to work on them for another 20 years. After many unsuccessful experiments the steam traction-engine began to find favour in the fifties and sixties ⟨160⟩. The first effective steamrollers were built by Aveling & Porter of Rochester in 1866–67; one of the earliest of them was continuously at work in Hull for 60 years.[75]

These vehicles were ponderous (an Aveling steamroller of 1866 acquired by the city of Liverpool weighed 30 tons) and they travelled extremely slowly. Any incentive to give them greater speed was removed by the passing of the Locomotives Act of 1861, which restricted them to 5 m.p.h. in towns and 10 m.p.h. on open roads in the country. Four years later these speeds were reduced to 2 and 4 m.p.h. respectively. These measures have often been ridiculed since. On this point they were indeed timid. One peer remarked, when the Bill of 1861 was under discussion, that 'the use of locomotives on common roads will give rise to dangerous accidents. Horses will be apt to take fright at them and human life may as a consequence be jeopardised.'[76] Yet these Acts were in truth the traction engines' charter, regulating their use as a normal form of transport and limiting the tolls they should pay on turnpike roads.

For them these speed restrictions were relatively unimportant. They totally inhibited, however, the development of mechanically-propelled vehicles for passengers and light freight. Moreover, though steam had been much used for moving passengers by road, it was unsatisfactory for this purpose, involving dirt and noise and constantly threatening explosion. Many efforts had already been made to discover a suitable substitute, both in Britain and on the Continent. It was in the 1880s, in Germany and France, that the internal combustion engine, consuming petrol as a fuel, was first used with success. Daimler and Benz, Panhard and Peugeot—all these historic manufacturing names had appeared by 1890. From Britain the chief early contribution came from J. B. Dunlop, who (improving on a device demonstrated by R. W. Thompson 40 years earlier) produced a pneumatic tyre in 1880. But British experiments with vehicles infringing the Act of 1865 were stopped or severely hampered by the local authorities.

Nevertheless, the motor car had powerful and persistent advocates, and

in 1896 they succeeded in persuading Parliament to amend the earlier
legislation so as to permit a maximum speed of 12 m.p.h. The manufacture
of cars now began as a serious business in Britain, establishing itself
notably in Coventry—already a centre of the bicycle industry—with the
Humber and the English Daimler companies. In 1895 F. W. Lanchester
began to produce his famous cars and Herbert Austin designed the first
Wolseleys. By 1903 the number of cars on the roads had grown so large
that registration became necessary. Under the Motor Car Act of that year
all cars had to be registered with local authorities, which were to assign
numbers to them. During the passage of the Bill the House of Lords showed
itself willing to abolish altogether the speed limit, but the Commons were
less bold and a compromise was reached whereby it was retained but
raised to 20 m.p.h.

In the first year of the new Act's operation 18,000 motor vehicles were
licensed. By 1913 123,000 motor cars, lorries, and taxis were at work in
Britain—not to mention motor cycles, goods vehicles (53,000 of them) and
army transport.[77] Motoring had become an accepted pastime. More than
that: the internal combustion engine was beginning to show its capacity
for commercial purposes. The first motor buses appeared in London in
1898–1903, and from 1905 onwards the General company engaged in a
series of large-scale experiments with a variety of types. After much
tribulation, for its passengers as well as for itself, the company achieved
success with the 'B' type of 1910 ⟨220⟩. These were wonderfully reliable
vehicles, of which some 4,000 were ultimately built. Their production enabled the General company to complete the mechanisation of its services
almost at once: its last horse-drawn bus ran in October 1911 ⟨221⟩. The
provinces lagged somewhat behind London. The Birmingham & Midland
Omnibus Company began motor services in 1904; it suspended them from
1907 to 1912. A number of railway companies took up the new form of
traction, primarily to feed their services in country districts, with intelligent foresight. But even though some of them invested quite heavily
in it, they did not persist. The Great Eastern Railway, for example, sold
off its buses to local operators in 1913.

Why was this development so irregular, launched with such enthusiasm
and then so haltingly carried forward? There are two main answers to that
question. The vehicles themselves could not yet be regarded as reliable.
Among buses the London 'B' remained uniquely successful; and though
dependable private cars were now appearing—headed by the Rolls-Royce
⟨217⟩—they required many facilities, for fuelling and maintenance and repair, that were not yet universally available. Motoring was still an adventure,
it had not yet become a matter of routine. Secondly, and more important,
the full development of the petrol-driven motor vehicle was retarded by

61

the state of the roads. The Local Government Acts of 1888 and 1894 reorganised their administration, with the effect of placing the main responsibility on the municipal, county, and rural district authorities. In theory the Local Government Board co-ordinated their efforts. In practice it did nothing of the kind. A Departmental Committee of the Board outlined a proposal for a national road policy in a report of 1903; the Board disregarded it. Without exaggeration it can be said that the central Government did nothing at all before 1909 to adapt the country's antiquated road system, developed for horses and foot travellers, to the demands of high-speed mechanical traction. All that was done in this direction was the work of local authorities under pressure from the new road-users' organisations, such as the Cyclists' Touring Club, developed out of an earlier body in 1883, the (Royal) Automobile Club of 1897, and the Automobile Association of 1905. It was, for example, through experiments conducted chiefly by these bodies and County Councils that the problem of dust on the roads was solved by the application of tar to their surfaces.

In 1909, however, the Government began to wake up to its responsibilities. It was not a President of the Local Government Board who showed a change of heart, but Lloyd George, who had just become Chancellor of the Exchequer. His famous Budget of that year included a proposal for the establishment of a Central Road Fund, to make grants to local authorities for the improvement of existing roads and to finance the construction of 'absolutely new' ones. Introducing the measure, Lloyd George pointed out that the administration of roads in England and Wales was divided among some 1,900 authorities, of which no less than 46 were concerned with the upkeep of the road from London to Carlisle alone. Now that the motor car had brought Carlisle within a summer day's driving of London, the absurdity of this arrangement became as plain as that of the multiplicity of turnpike trusts in the 1830s. Unfortunately, the clear administrative improvement entailed by Lloyd George's proposals was politically controversial: for to make the work of the Road Board effective it was necessary to give it power to acquire land compulsorily. Landowners, railway interests, even the Treasury (which disliked the plan on administrative grounds) joined in opposing the scheme, and, when it had been forced through Parliament, in hampering its effectiveness.

The Road Board undertook some valuable work. It initiated the building of the Croydon By-pass and the Great West Road; it helped to promote the construction of the rolling lift bridge over the Trent at Keadby that carried both the Great Central Railway and the road from Doncaster to Grimsby; it brought back into use some stretches of the Roman Foss Way between Newark and Lincoln. But useful though these measures were, they only tinkered with the problem. The Board was never able to formulate and carry into effect a national road policy for Britain.[78]

The first World War suspended this work. And at the same time it made the work much more urgently necessary. For that war brought the motor vehicle into its own, in a variety of forms: armoured car and tank, light car, lorry and bus. Whilst it is true that the war interrupted motor manufacture (most manufacturers went over to making munitions, the Wolseley company alone turning out three million shells), it familiarised hundreds of thousands of soldiers with the driving, maintenance, and potential use of motor vehicles, and the lessons it had taught were quickly applied in peace-time.

They became clear to every one in the 1920s. After a pause for breath at the close of the war, the motor industry surged forward. Between the first World War and the second the number of cars, taxis, and lorries registered in the United Kingdom rose as follows:

Aug. 1920	363,000
,, 1929	1,434,000
,, 1939	2,662,000

In the field of public transport the motor bus advanced steadily in the twenties and rapidly in the thirties. In London its development brought with it an acute problem of management. In the autumn of 1922 the old-established General company, which had enjoyed a virtual monopoly of the buses on the London streets, found itself in fierce competition with independent operators or 'pirates'.* It was still legally possible for any-body to run any licensed vehicle as a bus in London. The idea caught on, and the pirates had a merry time at the expense of the General. They ran only on the most profitable routes, at the most profitable times of the day; and since these were obviously the peak periods they greatly aggravated the already serious problem of traffic congestion. In 1924 the Government intervened, passing a Road Traffic Act that in effect prevented any new operators from coming in and did something to regulate those who were already at work. The pirates then began to sell out, often on favourable terms, to the General; and though in the summer of 1927 a number of them were amalgamated to form the London Public Omnibus company, before that year was over the new combine had come to terms with the General, providing that the two companies should co-ordinate their services on those roads on which both of them operated.

* This was not, as might be supposed, a rude term coined by the General; it was first applied to the independent operators by the secretary of their own Association of London Omnibus Proprietors.

63

The spectacular advance of the motor bus caused many provincial towns to wonder whether their tramways ought to be maintained. They still offered great advantages, above all in economy of operation; and in many towns the trams continued to grow in number and to carry an increasing traffic. The Tramways Committee of Manchester Corporation went into the question carefully in 1923 and reaffirmed its faith in trams. Motor buses, it said, should be used as far as possible as 'feeders' to tramway services, but the bus 'cannot be considered either as a practical or financial substitute for the tramcar for the passenger transportation of the city and districts, nor for the central area only'.[79] New construction continued in Manchester, and the tramway system there did not reach the peak of its development until 1929.

As the traffic in town streets increased, however, with the multiplication of motor vehicles, the inflexibility of the tramway grew more and more troublesome. If the double-deck tramcar could move a larger number of people—especially in hilly towns like Sheffield—than the motor bus of the twenties, it necessarily blocked the street to a much greater extent than its more manœuvrable rival. A vigorous attempt was made to develop another form of traction with some of the advantages of both: the trolley bus, tried out in the West Riding and London in 1911 ⟨210⟩ and developed with particular enterprise in Bradford during the succeeding 50 years. The advantages of the trolley-bus were substantial. Being trackless, it was a more flexible vehicle than the tram; its supply of power, from electricity, was more reliable than that of the still unpredictable petrol-driven bus. Many towns introduced trolley-buses in the twenties, side by side with trams or motor buses or both. Some, like Chesterfield and Ipswich, abandoned tramways entirely in favour of trolley-buses; whilst others, such as Burton-on-Trent, Dumbarton, and Greenock, adopted motor buses in complete substitution for trams. In the long run the advantages of the trolley-bus diminished in competition with its rivals. Even though trackless it was still dependent on fixed overhead transmission; and in the 1920s and 1930s the petrol and diesel-driven bus caught up with it in reliability. One merit, however, it has always retained beyond challenge. It is the most silent instrument of public transport. As we move into a noisier and noisier future, that is a substantial merit indeed.

No matter what form of traction they employed, the general experience of operators in these years agreed on one thing: that the business of public road transport was booming. This was true of many municipal undertakings. The number of passenger journeys made on Derby Corporation Transport was just over 18 million in 1919; it topped 40 million in 1939. It was even more strikingly true of private companies. Crosville Motor Services, for instance, which began operations with two buses in 1910, carried 1,800,000 passengers in 1919–20; in 1939–40 it carried 100,527,000. In large measure this represented the creation of new traffic: people took to riding where previously they had walked or cycled. But it also meant a successful robbing of traffic from the railways. In 1920 the railways carried 1,579 million passengers in the United Kingdom; by 1938 this had dwindled to 849 million. Their freight traffic fell off by 17 per cent in the same period.[80]

The explanation of the railways' decline is complex; it cannot be attributed solely to the development of motor transport. It was in part due to the first World War, in which they made a great contribution to victory that ran down their equipment and overstrained their resources. When the war was over, a new Ministry of Transport was formed, ostensibly to take care of the nation's interest in transport as a whole. The first Minister, Sir Eric Geddes, had been trained on the railways, and from the outset the road interests argued vociferously that successive Governments favoured the railways at their expense. A Railways Act of 1921 compulsorily amalgamated 120 small companies into four large units, the London, Midland & Scottish, the London & North Eastern, the Great Western, and the Southern Railways, leaving only the Underground system of London and some minor concerns out of the scheme. This did something to strengthen the railways, enabling them to put through some great and necessary improvements: most notably the electrification of the suburban system of the Southern, which extended by 1939 from London out to Chatham, Hastings, and Portsmouth. But essentially the railways remained on the defensive: their enterprise hampered by much out-of-date legislation, passed at a time when they enjoyed a near-monopoly of public transport, and inappropriate both to their situation and to the country's in the second quarter of the twentieth century.

The Ministry of Transport, with the backing of a determined Government, might possibly have remedied this disorder. What was wanted was a well-planned policy, integrating all forms of transport together and supplying adequate incentives to each to provide the service it was best fitted to afford. Very little of such planning took place, apart from the London Passenger Transport Act of 1933, which made a serious and on the whole successful attempt to co-ordinate road and rail transport in the most densely-populated region of the country. Otherwise the story is not one of co-ordination but of competition (which brought some benefit to the consumer and at the same time involved much social and economic waste), of ill-regulated efforts to hold a balance between rival interests, which in consequence brought every kind of pressure they could to bear upon public opinion, Parliament, and Government.

The railways and the roads were now competing vigorously over almost the whole field of transport, in the carrying of freight as well as of passengers. True, the railway remained supreme over the road in handling heavy merchandise like coal and steel. Its competitors in that field were still, as they had always been, the waterways and coastal shipping; and against them the railways held their own. But in all other kinds of freight haulage they had to meet increasingly severe competition from petrol- and diesel-driven road vehicles, which enjoyed some important advantages. As small units running on roads they had greater flexibility and could offer a service more exactly 'tailored' to the wishes of their customers; they could take their loads from door to door without the trans-shipment required by the railway; and they enjoyed freedom to fix their own charges, whereas the railways were restricted by rigid legislation, designed to protect the customer in the days of their near-monopoly and quite unsuitable now in the changed conditions of the 1920s and 1930s.

It is not surprising therefore that goods vehicles multiplied on the roads. With two exceptions they were not owned by large combines. The exceptions were the old-established firms of Pickford and Carter Paterson. As early as 1912 they had agreed to co-ordinate their services. By 1920 they were together operating 400 motor vehicles. Ten years later—following a precedent established by Pickford's nearly a hundred years before (see p. 49)—they both passed into the control of the main-line railway companies. Under the new management their business continued to expand, employing 3,000 vehicles by 1947. The characteristic road-haulage operator, however, was the small man owning only a few vehicles, perhaps one; and the last thing he would contemplate was selling out to the railways, his detested rivals.

The unrestricted competition of the twenties, however, in the long run benefited nobody; and in 1930 and 1933 legislation was passed that had some effect in curbing it. Under the Road and Rail Traffic Act of 1933 all goods vehicles had to be licensed, and the cost of licences was substantial. Very naturally, the operators complained bitterly of these measures, attributing them to the malign influence of the railways. Yet this legislation had some effects that were undoubtedly beneficent, particularly on the design of vehicles: for the method of taxation put a premium on ingenuity in reducing the ratio of tare to loaded weight and so encouraged British manufacturers to produce vehicles that were notably economical in operation.[81]

In the carrying of passengers the railways now had to meet road competition at every point. They continued to lose suburban traffic steadily to the trams and buses; the bus was proving a more flexible, and on the whole a more efficient, servant of rural communities; and even for long-distance travel, in which the railways had enjoyed an unchallenged supremacy since they snatched it from the coaches a hundred years before, fierce competition was beginning. The motor coach evolved from the charabanc, which became popular before the first World War ⟨216⟩. By the thirties it was running regular services from London to Glasgow and Edinburgh, to Liverpool and Wales and Cornwall, charging fares substantially lower than those of the railways. Many of these services were centralised in an imposing terminal station near Victoria, completed in 1932.

To this competitor the railways had two answers. Though they considered a general lowering of passenger fares impracticable, they introduced a greater range of reduced return tickets, many of them working out at the rate of a penny a mile, and they set themselves energetically to quicken and improve their express passenger services, to make the most of the one incontestable advantage they enjoyed over their rivals on the road, that of speed. The crown of their efforts in this direction came with the special high-speed services that were initiated by the London & North Eastern Railway in 1935 with its Silver Jubilee express running from King's Cross to Newcastle in four hours ⟨226⟩.

Yet the railways were fighting against very heavy odds. Their new triumphs in speed proved that they still enjoyed their old ascendancy over their rivals on the road. But a fresh competitor had now appeared, which commanded a speed greater than any the railways could hope to achieve: the aeroplane. In the twenties it had begun to make some small impression on the railways' profits from their cross-Channel services; now in the thirties it became a competitor within Britain itself ⟨230–2⟩. Not a serious one: for the unit was small, the charges it exacted were high, and much of its advantage in speed was lost, on short runs in Britain, owing to the time taken to drive to and from the airports. But the threat was clear enough. At yet another point the railways were on the defensive.

Such was their position when the second World War broke out in 1939. Like the rest of the transport industry, the railways rendered indispensable and priceless services to the country. But the war hit them disproportionately hard, not only by direct action through bombardment but also through the depreciation of their equipment. And immediately the war was over they became involved in furious political controversy. The Labour Government returned to power in 1945 was committed to a policy of nationalising transport; the Opposition was determined to fight the policy by every means in its power. The Government carried its measure in 1947. Under it the four main-line railway companies and the London Passenger Transport Board were nationalised, together with the waterways and the railway-owned docks. It had originally been intended to include, in addition, the whole of the long-distance road services. But here the Government gave ground, and in the event the new British Transport Commission acquired no more than a small portion of them.

From that time to this the nationalised railways have been a centre of political storms. The task of integrating them into one organisation was itself a large one, made more formidable by labour difficulties and shortages of material. No sooner was it beginning to show results than a change of Government brought modifications of the Act of 1947. In 1953 the Road Haulage Executive was abolished, and the effort made in the original Act to unify control of the whole transport system (tentative and imperfect as it had been) lapsed. Seven years later the Government decreed the winding-up of the British Transport Commission itself, the control over the railways having been decentralised in a steadily increasing measure since 1947.

At the same time successive Governments had recognised the desperate need of the railways for capital expenditure on a large scale to enable them to be re-equipped and brought up to date. The big Modernisation Plan of 1954 set out comprehensive and precise proposals, and the effects of it are now beginning to appear: in the rebuilding of stations, the construction of new marshalling yards, the superseding of steam by diesel and electric traction ⟨227–9⟩.

All this represents a new fighting back on the railways' part to hold and develop those services they are best qualified to provide. It is a fight not only against the operators of public transport on the roads. Equally—and, where passenger transport is concerned, much more seriously—it is a fight against the private car. At the outbreak of war in 1939 there were 2,662,000 cars, taxis, and lorries in Britain. By 1956 that number had more than doubled, to 5,527,000. Moreover, motor cycles, which had slumped in popularity in the thirties, had shown a striking return to favour, and there were now 1,239,000 of them. The railway strike of 1955 demonstrated the power of the motor vehicle: it showed that, for a limited time and in an emergency, the country could virtually dispense with the railway for its inland transport. And in the following year the Suez crisis showed, quite as plainly, how vulnerable the motor vehicle was if the supply of its fuel from the Middle East was disrupted.

The vast expansion of motor traffic concentrated attention more urgently than ever before on the inadequacy of the country's roads. Much was done in the thirties to improve the existing roads; and a little of this work—such as the Winchester By-pass—paid tribute to the techniques of building and layout that had revolutionised road construction in America and on the Continent. But each of these was a separate small operation. The country moved no nearer to a new road system, which was what it needed if it was to accommodate its rapidly growing number of motor vehicles. Even after the war, when that number was growing faster still, things moved very slowly. It was only in 1956 that the Government embarked on a plan involving the construction of new roads on a large scale: 'motorways', of which the first have now been brought into use ⟨237–8⟩. Coupled with the continued improvement of existing roads, even in remote parts of the country ⟨236⟩, this programme offers hope that we may come near to keeping pace with the growth of long-distance fast-moving traffic.

One effect of the new motorways, however, has been to emphasise even more strongly the hopeless inadequacy of the road system in our towns. The motorist who has driven steadily southward along M1 for 80 miles, in an hour or less, finds himself confronted with worse traffic jams than ever at the northern entrances to London. As yet we are operating only on the fringe of this problem. If we are to solve it we shall have to spend money on a scale hitherto unimagined and to plan in a way quite foreign to us. Two things equally vital are at stake: the ability to move the multitude of vehicles we manufacture, to enable them to give us the service they are designed for; and the preservation of our towns as habitable communities. The warning has been given to us, in memorable terms, by a modern town planner:

'It may be questioned whether the fundamental nature of the transport revolution has yet been grasped, whether it is appreciated that the advent of a means of personal mechanical locomotion adaptable for a host of everyday journeys has, by turning the streets into rivers of jostling, lethal vehicles, rendered out of date at a stroke the conventional arrangement of streets and buildings that has served us for so long. . . . The danger is that we may set our sights too low, that seeing the problem as no more than keeping traffic on the move we may take a middle course of piecemeal street widening with ever larger roundabouts, gradually tearing the hearts out of our towns. It is not traffic movement but civilised town life that is at stake.'[82]

It is right that this study should end with a question, an unsolved problem. For the history of transport is a history of changing conditions, new demands, and of the responses they have successively called forth.

1. The Roman road and its successors. Stane Street (running from Chichester to London) is seen here crossing Halnaker Hill in the parish of Boxgrove, Sussex. Going up from Chichester, the modern road (A285) takes the course of the Roman one, but at Warehead Farm (in the bottom left-hand corner of the picture) the two part: the Roman road runs on a characteristic bold course straight across the hill, its modern successor keeps level by skirting the base. Beyond the hill the two roads re-join for half a mile; and then the modern road turns to the left, making for Petworth, whilst Stane Street pursues its straight course (shown in the photograph) to Bignor and Pulborough.

A

2. A sailing-boat of the twelfth century; from a pictorial life of St. Guthlac, the founder of Crowland Abbey. Guthlac, having decided to establish himself as a hermit, is conveyed across the Fenland waters under the guidance of Tatwin. Sitting in the centre of the boat, he converses with Tatwin, who is in the stern steering by means of a paddle with a crutched handle. The rudder was not yet in use in this country. In the bows a man propels the boat with a punt-pole.

3. Seal of the borough of Ipswich. Its date is uncertain. Though the earliest surviving document to which it is affixed is of 1349, it seems to date from the granting of the first charter to the borough in 1200. If so, it gives the earliest British representation of a ship with a stern rudder: an important improvement introduced late in the twelfth century. The ship has 'castles' fore and aft – the word 'forecastle' is a survival from their use – providing raised accommodation for sailors, or for trumpeters and soldiers in a battle.

4. Rowing boat: from the *Luttrell Psalter*, *c.* 1340. The oarsmen appear to be singing, and to be pulling in the opposite direction from the men on the towrope. Is it a tug of war?

5, 6. Misericords in St. David's cathedral (second half of the fifteenth century). *Above*, shipwrights. The ship they are engaged on is clinker-built (i.e. with its planks overlapping, a fashion then just going out in Britain). *Below*, the ship at sea, propelled by an oar and steered with a stern rudder. This scene represents the passage of St. Govan on his way to Rome. His legend states that he nearly died of sea-sickness on the way; here he is seen in his agony.

7. Rhuddlan is a striking example, rare in this country, of an artificially created medieval port. Here Edward I built a new castle, and greatly extended the existing small town, in 1277–86. In 1277–80 the River Clwyd, which had hitherto wound a shallow and serpentine course over the alluvial flats to the sea, was straightened and canalised. This made Rhuddlan a port and enabled it to be used as the main English base of operations in the Welsh campaign of 1282. By the date of this picture (1795) a new harbour, for larger ships, had been developed at Foryd, at the mouth of the Clwyd, two miles away; but the river being tidal to a point above Rhuddlan, vessels of up to 70 tons' burthen could, and did, still sail up to the bridge.

8. The medieval bridge across the Tyne at Newcastle survived, unaltered in any important respect, until 1771, when it was broken down in a great flood. Its successor was completed in 1781; to be replaced in its turn by the swing bridge of 1876, which still stands, dwarfed by the high-level bridges on each side of it. The view in this picture is of unusual interest. It shows the fortified gateway at the north end of the medieval bridge; the large number of irregular houses built on it, as on London Bridge ⟨27⟩ and the Ouse Bridge at York; and, in the foreground, a couple of Newcastle keels, the flat-bottomed lighters used for loading colliers.

9. The medieval bridge at Dumfries, whose foundation is attributed to Devorguilla Balliol (d. 1290): from a drawing of 1747. The gateway between the third and fourth arches from the left marked the boundary between Nithsdale and Galloway; it was taken down about 1769, to lessen the weight on the bridge. The bridge is extant, somewhat altered, today, its nine arches reduced to six.

10. Huntingdon Bridge, one of the earliest major bridges to survive in this country. It dates from about 1300, replacing a predecessor largely destroyed by ice in the winter of 1293–4. It seems to have been erected by two authorities, whose work met in the middle. As the photograph shows, the piers of the bridge are triangular on the left and semi-hexagonal, with small triangular cutwaters, on the right. The third arch from the right was rebuilt, perhaps after the bridge had been damaged in the Civil War.

11. The Monnow Bridge at Monmouth is the only bridge in Great Britain that has retained to the present day a fortified tower on the bridge itself. The date of its construction is unknown, though it may date from the late thirteenth century. This water-colour drawing by Cornelius Varley, done in the early years of the nineteenth century, shows the bridge as it was when the tower was last occupied for defensive purposes – by troops charged with the defence of the county gaol in the Monmouthshire Rising of 1839. The ribbed construction of the bridge and its triangular cutwaters are well shown in the drawing. The bridge has been a little widened since then, but all traffic across it still passes under the arched gateway.

12. The bridge and lock at East Farleigh, near Maidstone: a perfect example of medieval bridge-building, dating probably from the fourteenth century. The section of the Medway between Maidstone and Tonbridge was made navigable under an Act of 1740.

13. Bideford Bridge, one of the longest medieval bridges surviving in this country. For its construction cf. p. 7.

14. The northern end of the bridge and causeway at Abingdon, built in 1416–37 (see pp. 11-12).

Et iusticia illius in filios filiorū: hiis qui seruant testamentum eius. Et memores sunt mandatorum ipsius: ipsius: ad faciendum ea.

15, 16. Though these two pictures, from the *Luttrell Psalter*, are very well known, and though a satirical purpose can be seen in each, they deserve respect as careful delineations of the wheeled vehicles of the fourteenth century. It is noticeable that the coach (*above*) is for the use of ladies – perhaps, from their coronets, queens – only, attended by men on horseback, one of whom is taking a pet monkey from the lady at the back. The cart (*below*) is depicted in great detail, down to its studded wheels and the hooves of its horses.

truristi omnes sepes eius: posu

17, 18, 19.

In 1517 John Greenway, who had made a fortune in the cloth trade, added an aisle to the south side of Tiverton church. Its exterior is elaborately decorated, in part with sculpture representing the means by which he had acquired his wealth: wool-packs, staple marks, anchors (seen at the bottom of the upper photograph, above a window), and ships. The ships are carved with extraordinary verve. Their construction, their rigging and equipment, and their crews are represented in minute detail, much of it wonderfully preserved.

20, 21, 22.

Ships sometimes figure on bench-ends in churches in the maritime parts of the country. That at East Budleigh, Devon (*left*), is elaborate and depicts an early three-masted ship, with the fortifications of a harbour in the background. At Bishops Lydeard, Somerset (*above*), the representation is cruder. At St. Winnow, Cornwall (*opposite page*), a two-masted ship is shown in a storm, with the terrified crew gazing up to heaven and a face peering at them out of the clouds – perhaps God the Father looking to their safety. The East Budleigh carving may have been executed about 1500; the others date from later in the sixteenth century.

23. By the late sixteenth century the full-rigged ship had developed into a large and complex craft. This is the *Ark Royal*, one of the largest ships in the navy of Elizabeth I. The 'castles' are now reduced in proportionate size and incorporated as permanent features of the ship. At the stern the gallery has appeared, which grew into a prominent, and lavishly decorated, element in the ships of the seventeenth and eighteenth centuries.

24. Gravesend was incorporated as a borough by charters of Elizabeth I in 1562 and 1568. One of the grounds stated in the preamble to the charter of 1562 was that 'the common passage by water between Gravesend and London . . . is not rightly governed.' This passage, generally known as 'The Long Ferry', was indeed of great economic importance to Gravesend. It was the first of three regular recognised stages in a journey between London and the Continent: the Long Ferry, road from Gravesend to Dover, boat from Dover to Calais. The Elizabethan arms granted for the use of the portreeve of the borough depict a sailing ship rowed by five men and steered by a porcupine: a design with a double purpose, to give prominence to the Long Ferry and to refer to the patronage of Sir Henry Sidney, the porcupine being the Sidneys' device.

25. The 'Long Ferry' was regulated jointly by the municipal authorities of London and Gravesend, and all breaches of the rules that governed it were dealt with by a court held by the lords of the manor of Gravesend. Here is part of the court roll for 1595. It lays down that no tilt-boat (i.e. rowing boat with an awning—the type used on the Long Ferry), 'of what bigness soever the same be, shall carry at one time above thirty passengers over and above the watermen that row and the steersman and shall be rowed with five oars at the least, and shall not be overmasted or sailed whereby the passenger shall be in danger of drowning, which tilt-boat for herself, the steersman, and five watermen shall be allowed for one such passage fifteen shillings and no more.' The penalty for carrying more than 30 passengers was to be a fine of 30s.

26. One of the finest surviving examples of Elizabethan bridge-building: Wilton Bridge, spanning the Wye ¾ mile west of Ross. It was built in 1597–9, and when it was completed Charles Bridges was authorised to levy tolls on those using it in compensation for the loss of his rights in the ferry it replaced. The design of the bridge reflects interesting differences from medieval practice. The arches have now become rounded, and though they are ribbed underneath the ribbing seems more a decorative than a structural feature. The far end of the bridge, on the Hereford side, was demolished during the Civil War and rebuilt afterwards.

27. This enlargement of a section of a painting of old London Bridge by Claude de Jongh, dated 1630, gives a good impression of the houses piled, up to a height of four storeys, on top of it. It also shows the 'starlings', the wooden piles protecting the piers, and a characteristic group of river craft, including two state barges.

8 The High Bridge at Lincoln is one of the few that still carry buildings. The medieval stone arches remain. The four-storied superstructure dates from the early sixteenth century, much 'restored' and altered in the nineteenth.

B

29. Carved panel at the south end of Tolbooth Wynd, Leith, depicting the import of wine (1678). On the left is a two-masted sailing-ship, complete with lee-boards and anchor. On the right is the warehouse on the quay, with a crane landing casks of wine. The rope is hauled up by a boy working a treadmill. In the top left-hand corner two wine porters are carrying a cask slung from a pole; this method of carriage was called 'sting and ling', and wine-porters were thence known as 'sting-men'.

30. New Aberdeen at the end of the seventeenth century. (Old Aberdeen, with the spires of the cathedral, is seen on the extreme right.) This engraving gives a good impression of a port before the improvements of the great eighteenth-century engineers began. All that has been done is to build a small breakwater at the mouth of the Dee, with a blockhouse on the opposite bank for defence and a quay where the main channel of the river narrows. When Smeaton and Telford created the modern port of Aberdeen they experienced great difficulties from shifts in the river and its banks.

31, 32, 33.

Wagons at Cambridge, from Loggan's *Cantabrigia Illustrata* (*c.* 1690). *At the top* a hay-cart, with a haymaker asleep on the load. *In the middle* a brewers' dray. *At the bottom* a stage wagon, with two passengers sitting in front. This was the normal means of public transport over long distances for those who could not afford the high fares charged by the coaches.

A Citicen riding with his Wife. 54

34.

The ordinary mode of travel in the early seventeenth century continued to be on horseback. This drawing shows a London citizen, with his wife riding pillion and side-saddle behind.

COACH and SEDAN,
Pleafantly Difputing for Place and Precedency
The *Brewers-Cart* being Moderator.

Spectatum admiffi, rifum teneatis amici?

Dudgin   Powell

LONDON: *1636*
Printed by *Robert Raworth*, for *Iohn Crowch*; and are to be fold
Edmund Paxton, dwelling at *Pauls* chayne, neere Doctors-Commons. 16

35.

The sedan chair was introduced into England from the Continent, probably in the 1620s. In 1634 Sir Saunders Duncombe was granted a monopoly of the provision of these chairs for hire, and they became popular for a little while. Later in the century a wheeled version of the chair appeared, somewhat like the Chinese rickshaw (there is an example in the Maidstone Museum of Carriages). In the eighteenth century the sedan chair became an elegant object, a standard instrument of public transport in all large towns ⟨71⟩. The chair shown here is one of the earliest (1636), resembling a hut carried on poles. The coach, its rival, is octagonal in shape, and the passengers are enabled to see out only by lowering a flap in the side. The 'glass coach' did not come in until the next generation.

36. This picture (again from Loggan's *Cantabrigia Illustrata*) gives a good notion of the cumbrous design of the seventeenth-century coach, dragged by six horses and accompanied by a man on foot.

37. The murder of Thomas Thynne in Pall Mall by Capt. Vratz, at the instigation of the Swede Count John Philip Königsmark, in 1682: relief from Thynne's monument in Westminster Abbey, by Arnold Quellin. An early representation of the smaller coach of lighter construction, known as a chariot, which began to become fashionable in Charles II's reign.

38, 39. Two of the lighter coaches, or 'chariots', whose use developed late in the seventeenth century. That shown above was made for the Baskerville family and retains much of its original leather decoration. The lower picture shows the coach made for the Trewinnard family, said to be the first coach seen in Cornwall. Both depend for their springing on stout leather straps suspended from the upper cross-bars of the frame.

40. Of the series of over 60 plates representing the towns and great houses of Scotland in Slezer's *Theatrum Scotiae* (1693), only four show coaches. This view of Falkland Palace is evidently intended to portray the arrival of a group of distinguished visitors: the nearest coach, indeed, is drawn by six horses, an extravagance uncommon at the time even in wealthier England. That in the background on the left is drawn by four horses; the one on the right, which is the smallest, by two.

41. A specimen of the simple horse-drawn sledge used widely in Scotland before the spread of wheeled vehicles in the eighteenth and early nineteenth centuries and in the Highlands almost down to the present day. The under-frame of this sledge (depicted in front of Dunblane cathedral) is fixed to two long timbers, which also form the shafts for the horse; and it is raised on two supports, running at an oblique angle and trailing along the ground. A similar sledge is shown in Slezer's picture of Arbroath, but this lacks the trailing supports.

Lincolnshire.

	Lincolne	Grantham	Beckingham	Gaynsburgh	Burton	Barton	Market Rasen	Horne Castle	Bullingbrooke	Spilsby	Wayne-fleete	Boston	Quaploade	Spalding	Crowland	Market Deeping	Bourne	Folkingham	Stamforde	Alforde	Dunnington	Lowthe	Salt-fleete	Thongcaster	Grymsby	Great Limbergh	Kirton in Lindsey
Sleeforde.	14	9	10	26	38	42	24	15	17	19	23	15	17	14	18	17	13	5	18	25	8	24	29	30	34	29	30
Kirton in lindes.	15	33	25	7	14	13	10	20	25	27	32	31	40	38	44	43	38	31	51	27	32	19	23	9	16	10	
Great Limbergh	20	36	28	17	13	8	9	19	22	23	28	21	42	40	47	47	42	35	47	21	33	13	15	4	6		
Grymsbye.	22	38	32	23	18	13	12	18	20	20	25	29	40	40	46	47	43	36	49	18	34	10	10	8			
Thongcaster.	16	32	25	15	14	11	6	16	20	20	26	27	37	36	43	43	38	31	44	20	30	11	14				
Salte-fleete.	24	38	33	29	28	22	44	14	14	13	16	23	34	35	42	43	39	33	45	9	29	6					
Lowthe.	20	32	27	28	25	21	10	9	11	11	15	19	30	31	37	38	34	28	41	9	25						
Dunnington.	22	15	18	31	41	41	24	16	16	17	19	8	9	7	13	14	11	7	17	23							
Alforde.	23	33	31	31	34	29	17	11	8	6	7	15	26	28	35	37	33	28	39								
Stamforde.	36	14	22	40	52	54	38	32	32	34	35	25	18	14	10	5	7	13									
Folkingham.	18	8	13	28	40	42	25	19	17	22	25	15	14	10	14	12	8										
Bourne.	26	12	19	35	48	49	32	25	25	27	29	19	13	8	8	5											
Market deeping.	31	16	23	40	52	53	37	29	30	30	32	21	13	10	5												
Crowland.	33	20	27	42	53	54	37	29	28	29	29	19	9	7													
Spalding.	26	17	23	37	48	48	31	22	21	22	22	13	4														
Quaploade.	38	21	26	39	49	48	32	22	20	20	20	11															
Boston.	21	22	23	32	40	38	22	12	9	10	11																
Wayntfleete.	26	32	31	35	40	36	22	12	7	5																	
Spilsbye.	20	28	26	29	35	31	17	7	3																		
Bullingbrooke.	18	26	24	28	33	30	16	5																			
Horne Castle.	14	24	20	23	29	27	11																				
Market Rasen.	10	27	20	14	18	17																					
Barton.	28	42	34	19	8																						
Burton.	24	39	30	14																							
Gaynsburgh.	12	26	17																								
Beckingham.	10	9																									
Grantham.	18																										

The vse of this Table.

THe Townes or places betweene which you desire to know, the distance you may finde in the names of the Townes in the vpper part and in the side, and bring them in a square as the lines will guide you: and in the square you shall finde the figures which declare the distance of the miles.

And if you finde any place in the side which will not extend to make a square with that aboue, then seeking that aboue which will not extend to make a square, and see that in the vpper, and in the side, and it will showe you the distances. It is familiar and easie.

Beare with defectes, the vse is necessarie.

Inuented by IOHN NORDEN.

VVHere iournyes lye ouer the Fennes and Washes, the distances are vncertaine, for that they be more passable in the Summer then in the Winter, and at all times curuing, and longer or shorter.

42. A distance table from John Norden's *Intended Guide for English Travellers* (1625): the first appearance of a device still in use at the present day. Notice the caution at the foot, very necessary in Lincolnshire, concerning journeys made over 'fens and washes'.

43. When John Ogilby published his *Britannia* in 1675, he wrought a revolution in map-making in this country. For his were the first maps to be devoted primarily to roads, showing details of their topography to a scale of one inch to a mile. He claimed that they were based on 'actual dimensuration', and the instrument he used for measuring them was a 'way-wiser' like that shown in this figure from his book. An eighteenth-century way-wiser is to be seen in the Cornwall County Museum, Truro.

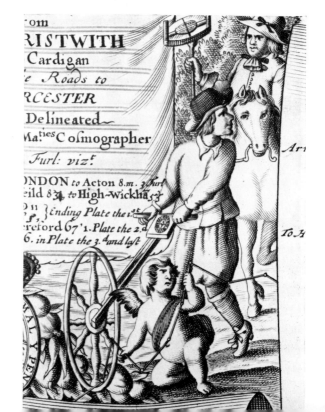

4. Part of the title-page of Ogilby's *Britannia*, engraved by Hollar, showing details of life on the roads to be seen in his time. The two horsemen issuing from the gateway and the group seated in the foreground on the left are carrying Ogilby's strip maps.

45 Artificially straight roads were rare in this country between the time of the Romans and our own century, when new motor roads are being built. The Long Walk at Windsor is one of the few exceptions. Laid out in 1680–4, it was designed for pleasure and did not carry a heavy traffic, though in George I's time the 'nobility, gentlemen, and inhabitants' of the neighbourhood found it so useful that they petitioned the king that it should be kept in good repair. The colossal bronze statue of George III, which stands at the end of the walk on Snow Hill (seen at the foot of the picture), was erected in 1831, terminating the sweeping view southward from the castle.

Anno Sexto

Annæ Reginæ.

An Act for Repairing the Highways from *Old Stratford* in the County of *Northampton,* to *Dunchurch* in the County of *Warwick.*

Hereas the Ancient Road between the Cities of London and Westchester, (and now and for many Years last past, the Common Post-Road towards Ireland) is so very Ruinous and almost Unpassible for above Twenty two Miles in length, from a Place called the Saracen's-Head Inn in Old-Stratford in the County of Northampton, to the Town of Dunchurch in Warwickshire, that it is become dangerous to all Persons that pass those Ways; and for that the ordinary Course appointed by the Laws of this Realm now in force, are not sufficient for the effectual Repairing and Amending the same; and for that the Inhabitants of the several Parishes in which the said Ruinous Roads do respectively lye, are not able to Repair the same, without some other Provision, there being no Materials for the Amendment thereof to be had, but at great distance from the said respective Places: For Remedy whereof, and to the intent the same may be speedily and effectually Amended and kept in good Repair, may it please Your Majesty that it may be Enacted; and be it Enacted by the Queens most Excellent Majesty, by and with the Advice and Consent of the Lords Spiritual and Temporal, and the Commons in this present Parliament Assembled, and by the Authority of the same, That it shall be in the Power of Sir John Mordant, Sir Justinian Isham, Sir Thomas Cave, Sir William Boughton, Sir John Shuckburgh, Sir Pope Danvers, Sir Fuller Skipworth, Sir Orlando Bridgeman, Sir William Wheeler, Sir Thomas Wagstaffe, Sir John Whitwrong, Baronets; Sir Robert Clerke Knight, William Bromley, Thomas Cartwright, Andrew Archer, George Mountague, Francis Arundell sen. Francis Arundell jun. Lucy Knightly, Charles Howe, Edward Stratford, William Ward, Bazill Feilding, William Palmer, Robert Harvey, Nicholas Breton, Symon Biddolph, William Boughton, Thomas Viner, Toby Chancy sen. Thomas Lister, Thomas Trist, Henry Longueville, Joseph Ashley, Edward Bagshaw, John Hastings, John Creswell Wentworth, William Ives, Robert Andrew, John Parkhurst, Thomas Thornton, Henry Benson, Arthur Gregory, John Astley, William Westley, Knightly Danvers, Brown Willis, John Winston, Thomas Hiccock, Nathaniel Parkhurst, Allen Bathurst, George Boon, Henry Neale, Edward Hopkins,

A 2   Francis

46. The first page of an early Turnpike Act (1708) for repairing the road from Old Stratford, on the north bank of the Ouse opposite Stony Stratford, to Dunchurch, near Rugby. As far as Weedon this road formed part of the Roman Watling Street. As the Act recites, it was the main road from London to Chester and 'the common post-road towards Ireland'. The Act authorises the erection of two turnpikes across this section of road, for the collection of dues at stipulated rates during the 21 years following. It appoints 74 named trustees for the execution of the work, all country gentlemen of Northamptonshire and Warwickshire – prudently putting their quorum, however, as low as five.

48. Dunston Pillar, the land lighthouse erected at the expense of Sir Francis Dashwood in 1751 to guide travellers from Sleaford across the wild heath into Lincoln. This was a stretch of country notorious for highwaymen. By 1810 it no longer served its original purpose, and a statue of George III was substituted for the light on top, in commemoration of the king's jubilee.

47. The term 'highwayman' was coined in the seventeenth century to denote a new and formidable kind of robber, who depended for his livelihood upon the increasing movement of travellers along the roads. The first of them to become celebrated was Claude Duval (1643–70), a Norman by birth, who came over to England at the Restoration. During the succeeding ten years he enjoyed a reputation both for his robberies and for his gallantry to women. He was captured, drunk, in 1670 and executed. This picture represents Duval's robbery of Mr. Roper, Master of the Buckhounds to Charles II, in Windsor Forest. Though drawn nearly a century afterwards, it is interesting as an example of the later romanticising of Duval's trade. It comes from a collection of *Lives of the Highwaymen*.

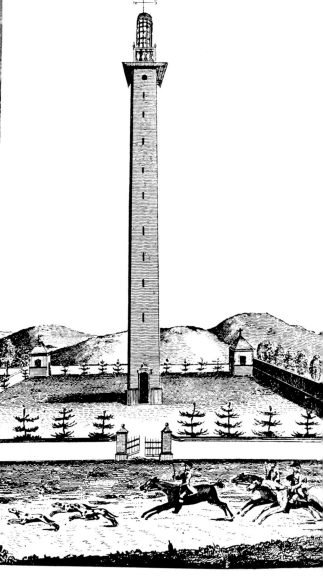

49, 50.

Signposts began to be erected systematically on the roads in the seventeenth century, though few have survived from that date. In the North of England, where stone was plentiful, they frequently took the form of square standing pillars. Two of these are illustrated here. That *above*, of 1738, is at Farnley Moor End on the old road from Huddersfield to Penistone, specifying the names of the Constable and the Surveyor. *Below*, a turnpike guidepost of the same form at Rastrick, Yorks. (W.R.). 'Junction' is the settlement of Denshaw, where five roads met (and still meet), close to the Lancashire border on the descent into Oldham. The road on which this guidepost stands was built under an Act of 1806. The post is a rarity because the stone-cutter has carved his name on it and because it is an individually-designed stone, not one of a standard series as normally set up by the turnpike trusts.

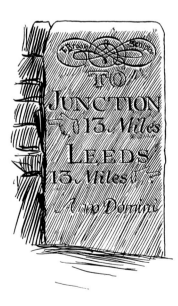

1. Ralph Allen (1694–1764), who made a well-earned fortune out of the development of postal services in the English provinces between 1720 and 1764.

2. State barge made for Frederick, Prince of Wales, in 1732: the finest boat of its date to survive in Britain. The decoration was designed by William Kent, the carving was executed by James Richards, the painting and gilding by Paul Pettit. There are seats for 21 oarsmen and for up to 9 passengers in the cabin.

53. The Bridge of Tay at Aberfeldy, Perthshire, completed in 1733 under the direction of General George Wade: a striking monument of Wade's patient and productive years superintending the building of military roads and bridges in the Highlands.

54. Smeaton's bridge over the Tay at Perth, built in 1766–71, to replace that destroyed in the flood of 1621 (see p. 14). The overhanging footway and its parapet are an addition of 1869.

. The earliest known railway bridge: Causey Arch, built in 1727 at the substantial cost of £12,000 to carry a wagon way over Causey Burn near Tanfield, Co. Durham. The mason who built it was named Ralph Wood. When this drawing was made, at the beginning of the nineteenth century, the bridge was already falling into disuse. It survives, however, as a ruin to the present day and is, rightly, scheduled for preservation by the Ministry of Works.

. The bridge of Pontypridd. It was the work of a local man, William Edwards, who undertook to build and maintain a bridge over the Taff in 1746. His first bridge was of three arches, and it was destroyed in a flood two years later. Next he built one of a single span (1751), but the keystone was unable to resist the pressure of the abutments and the bridge collapsed. At his third attempt he therefore lightened the abutments by piercing them with holes. The method was successful, and the bridge has stood from its completion in 1755 to the present day. It was never a very convenient structure because of its steep pitch; and heavily-laden vehicles continued to ford the river whenever possible.

C

57, 58. The first bridge successfully built of cast-iron
has given its name, Ironbridge, to the industrial settlement it served, spanning the Severn
close to Coalbrookdale. It was designed by
Abraham Darby and brought into use in 1779.
It is now closed to wheeled traffic and is protected as an ancient monument.

. Stourport sprang up like a mushroom with the opening of the Staffordshire and Worcestershire Canal in 1772 (see p. 34). It enjoyed three-quarters of a century of prosperity and then began a slow decline, which has made it a quiet place today. This view shows part of the main canal basin and a handsome warehouse (now converted into a sawmill).

60. The canal frontage of another warehouse. Its upper storeys are built out on eight iron columns.

. The Tontine Hotel, Stourport, with lock and toll-house in the foreground. The name of the hotel proclaims the means by which its building was financed.

62. Most canal bridges were built of brick, their design plain, but reflecting the elegance natural to their time. This bridge spans the Staffordshire & Worcestershire Canal at its junction with the Trent & Mersey at Great Haywood, Staffs.

63. Entrance to the Sapperton Tunnel, on the Thames & Severn Canal. This tunnel (3,817 yards long) was built in 1784–9 and was then the longest and widest tunnel in this country. The *Annual Register* hailed the completion of the canal as effecting 'the greatest object of internal navigation in this kingdom'. Such rejoicing proved to be premature, for the canal suffered from the defects of navigation on the two great rivers it linked, and in later years from the competition of two other canals, the Kennet & Avon and the Wilts. & Berks., and of the Great Western Railway. The tunnel was disused in 1911, and almost the whole canal was abandoned in 1927.

64. Slate tablet on a toll bridge. This stood on the Cavendish Bridge, erected about the middle of the eighteenth century to take the main road from London to Derby and Manchester across the Trent. The bridge was broken down in the great frost of 1947 and has now been replaced; but the Leicestershire County Council has happily preserved this relic of the old bridge beside the road.

119]	ROADS measured from HICK's HALL.	[120

Rudland		5	211¼
Abergeley,	Denb.	5	216¼

LONDON to *Bangor* and *Holyhead, by Shrewsbury.*

To *Shrewsbury,* p. 123			154
Montford Bridge		4	158
Enfdon		2	160
Neffcliff		2½	162½
Ofweftry		9½	172
Llangollen,	Denb.	12	184
Corwen		12	196
Kenniogga		13	209
Llanrooft		11	220
Conway		12	232
Bangor Ferry		17	249
Crofs to Anglefea			
Gwyndy		12½	261½
Holyhead		12½	274

N. B. The above is hard, smooth, level Road, and extremely pleafant. A Coach goes conftantly the above Road from Shrewsbury, it being paffable at all Times.

One Mile on the r. beyond Shrewfbury, fee acrofs the Severn, Berwick, Thomas Jeif Powis, Efq.
At 14½, on the l. is Afton, Rev. Mr. Lloyd.
On the l. about four Miles beyond Ofweftry, is Chirk Town and Caftle, the Seat of Richard Myddleton, Efq.
Near Clangollen, on the r. is Caftle Dinas Brane, famous in Hiftory.
About two Miles from Llangollen, on the r. are the Ruins of a very large Abbey, well worth the Notice of the curious in Antiquity.
About a Mile farther, on the r. are the Ruins of the Palace of Owen

Glyndwr; and alfo Llanfillio, the Seat of Thomas Jones, Efq.
About a Mile farther, on the right, the Village of Llan St. Fraid.
On the r. Half a Mile this Side of Caer y' Drudion, is the famous Citadel of the Druids, whereto Characacus retired after his Defeat at Caer Caradoc.
Between Corwen and Keniogge-Mawr is a famous Stone Cheft of the Druids; near Kenioge, the Seat of —— Kenryck, Efq.
At Llanrwft is a Bridge over the River Conway, built by Inigo Jones, and faid to be his Mafter-Piece.
On the left of Llanrwft is Gweder, a Seat of the Duke of Ancafter.

Another Road to Holyhead, viz.

To Northorp, p. 116			193
Cravatelough		1½	194½
The Smelt Mills		5½	200
Pontriffith Br.	Denb.	5	205
Denbigh		3	208
Hen Llan		2½	210½
Llanwith		3½	214
Pontgwithy Bridge		2	216
Bettws		3	219
Dolven Bridge & Mill		1½	220½
Crofworth		6	226½
Conway Ferry		1½	228
Abercomvay,	Caern.	¾	228¾

When the tide is out, keep to the r. over a Skirt of Penman-Vechan Mountain; and along the Sands to Meney Straits, where you ferry over to

Beaumaris,	Angl.	12	240¾
Tincohet		5¼	246
Hildravaught Mill		3½	249½
Llangaveney		1½	251

65.

Toll-house at Littleborough, Notts., on the road from Lincoln to Doncaster. These buildings were frequently, like this one, octagonal, with windows in the splayed walls and at the sides to give the tollkeeper a clear view up and down the road. It was important that he should move as quickly as possible to take his toll and open the gate.

66.

As more people took to travelling by road in the eighteenth century, guidebooks multiplied for their use. Among the most famous were the road-books produced by John Cary and Daniel Paterson in a long series of editions between 1771 and 1832. Here is a page from Paterson's *New and Accurate Description of all the . . . Roads in England and Wales* (9th ed., 1792) describing the roads to Holyhead before Telford began to work on them.

67, 68. The effort to produce lighter and faster vehicles holding a smaller number of passengers continued. (*Above*) The Baskerville phaeton of 1698, designed for two passengers only. (*Below*) The Lister post-chaise, 1725, providing more substantial cover but less ponderous and roomy than the coach. It was driven not from a box but by a postillion riding one of the horses.

69. John Wood's Sudbury, Hedingham & Braintree coach, *c.* 1800. Notice the passengers accommodated in the boot. The background of mountains is somewhat fanciful for Essex; but the artist (who was probably a coach-builder by trade) has rendered the coach and its passengers with close fidelity.

70. This print of the entrance to the Theatre Royal, Drury Lane, gives some impression of the crowding of eighteenth-century streets by coaches, sedan chairs, and horses. By this date (1776) the decoration both of chairs and of carriages was at its most elegant.

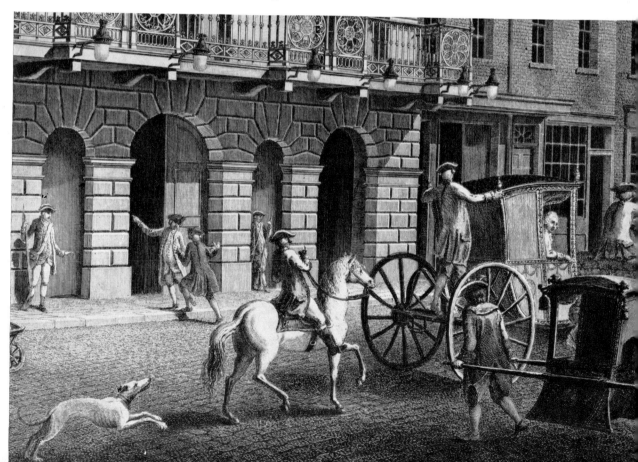

71. It is not easy to get a clear impression of the appearance of a country turnpike road in the eighteenth century before the improvements of Telford and McAdam. The purpose of this drawing, made in 1780 by S. H. Grimm, was to depict the ruins of the medieval manor-house of Poynings on the Sussex Downs; but it also shows the Brighton-Henfield turnpike road very clearly in the foreground. To judge from the colour of the drawing the road had been generously metalled, for it shows none of the chalky whiteness that would be natural here; but the surface is far from smooth, and storms of rain on these steep hills must have riven gullies in it. Notice the wide grass verge, still useful for enabling detours to be made when the road was deeply rutted. The chalk bank on the left indicates that the level of the road had been lowered: probably an improvement due to the turnpike trust.

72. Raised 'causey', Throstle Nest Lane, Bradley, Huddersfield. The stone-paved causey provided a hard track that could be used all the year round by packhorses, carrying wool and cloth in single file.

73.

Silver cup presented by Glasgow Chamber of Commerce to John Palmer in grateful recognition of his services in establishing the mail coach from 1784 onwards.

74.

The White Hart, Salisbury: one of the more splendid products of the coaching age. Note the fine pair of hexagonal iron lanterns. The hotel belongs to Trust Houses Ltd., a company formed in 1919 and now owning over 200 hotels throughout Great Britain.

75. The royal mails at the Angel, Islington, on George IV's birthday, 1828. On the evening of the king's birthday the 28 mail coaches that left London every night made a tour of the capital from Lincoln's Inn Fields to St. James's Palace, where the coachman of the Bristol mail (the senior service) proposed the king's health. This print shows the Liverpool mail just starting, with the Manchester and Holyhead coaches ready to leave.

77. Mail coach, *c.* 1820. Coaches of this type made the fastest runs ever achieved with horse traction. ▶ Some examples are still to be seen: e.g. the Devonport Mail of 1835, in the Hull Transport Museum, and the York Mail of 1840, in the Maidstone Museum of Carriages.

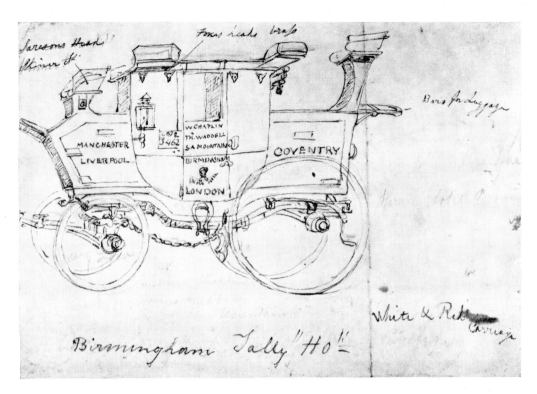

Saracens Head
Skinner St

Foxes heads brass

Bars for luggage

White & Rich Carriage

MANCHESTER
LIVER POOL

W.CHAPLIN
Tn.WADDELL
S.A.MOUNTAIN
BIRMINGHAM
LONDON

COVENTRY

Birmingham Tally "Ho!"

76. Rough sketch by James Pollard of the Birmingham Tally Ho! coach, one of those controlled by
William Chaplin. Note his careful attention to the mechanism of the springing and to such details
as the bars for luggage under the guard's seat at the back and the brass foxes' heads on either side of
the door.

78. This rustic bridge near Cyfarthfa, comprising the branch of a tree and a rude ladder, caught the eye of J. C. Ibbetson when he was sketching in South Wales. The industrialisation of the valley had already begun, and only a short distance away, in Cyfarthfa itself, the iron works were already established that were to yield millions to the Crawshays, their proprietors, and good employment for many years to the rapidly-multiplied population of Merthyr Tydfil and its neighbourhood.

79. The majority of bridges in Britain remained of timber until the nineteenth century. This is a drawing of Windsor Old Bridge made by J. Buckler in 1810. It was replaced by an iron bridge in 1822–4.

0. A ferry boat (1802). This shows the type of broad, flat-bottomed boat that had developed in response to the demands of increasingly heavy wheeled traffic. A large covered waggon is being loaded on to the boat, the horse having preceded it. The ferryman sits by apathetically.

1. The ferry across the Tamar at Saltash, Cornwall (1822). Brunel's Royal Albert Bridge (completed in 1859) crosses the river at this point, the railway curving away to the left at a high level. A road bridge has now been built immediately adjacent to the railway bridge. A steam ferry continues to operate.

82. Breaking stones by hand for road-making in Yorkshire. Print dated 1813.

83. Welsh drovers crossing a river with their cattle. From a coloured print by George Baxter (1804–67).

34. Highland drovers near Inveraray, by Joshua Cristall (*c.* 1767–1847). The over-dramatised landscape may represent Glen Kinglas, up which an important drove road ran between Inveraray and Arrochar. This was the route taken by many of the droves of sheep and cattle from Islay, Jura, and Kintyre to the great Trysts at Falkirk, which displaced Crieff as the main market about 1770.

85. This portrait of John Loudon McAdam (1756–1836) emphasises the rugged force of the engineer. He hailed from Ayrshire and became interested in the improvement of roads through serving as a magistrate and road trustee in his own county. He became Surveyor-General of the Bristol roads in 1815 and proceeded to put his devices into practice. 'Macadamising', 'Tarmacadam' and hence 'Tarmac' are all words derived from his name.

86. Thomas Telford (1757–1834). Portrait painted by Samuel Lane in 1822 for the Institution of Civil Engineers, of which he was the first President. The Pontcysyllte Aqueduct appears in the background. When this portrait was painted in 1822 Telford was at the height of his fame: the Caledonian Canal was completed in this year, and he was nearing the end of his work on the Holyhead road and the Göta Canal in Sweden.

87. The Chirk Aqueduct on the Shropshire Union Canal, designed by Telford and completed in 1801. This drawing of three of the ten arches was made by J. S. Cotman from a sketch taken on a tour into North Wales in the summer of 1802. The aqueduct lies across the boundary between Shropshire in England and Denbighshire in Wales.

88, 89.
Above, the surface of the canal with the tunnel at the northern end of the aqueduct; *below*, the aqueduct now overshadowed by the taller viaduct of the Great Western Railway, crossing the River Ceiriog at the same point.

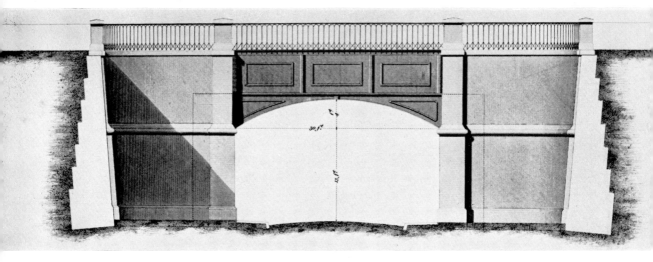

90. Aqueduct carrying the Birmingham & Liverpool Junction Canal over the main London-Chester road near Nantwich. The bridge itself is of iron, the curved abutments of masonry. Notice the simplicity and elegance of the railings. This was Telford's last great work, completed in 1835, six months after his death.

91. The Brynich Aqueduct (engineer, Thomas Dadford), completed in 1800 to carry the Brecknock & Abergavenny Canal over the Usk 2 miles east of Brecon.

92. Top lock of the flight of 5 at Allt-yr-yn, Newport, on the Monmouthshire Canal, completed *c.* 1796.

93. The flight of 29 locks on the Kennet & Avon Canal at Devizes, completed in 1810. This 'staircase' raises the level of the canal from the valley of the Bristol Avon to the Vale of Pewsey. In 1829 these locks were lit by gas to enable them to be negotiated by night.

94. Muirtown locks on the Caledonian Canal (cf. p. 35). A Dutch vessel leaving with a cargo of timber.

95. Mountford Bridge, carrying the Holyhead road over the Severn 5 miles west of Shrewsbury. This bridge was built to the designs of Thomas Telford in 1790–2, from red sandstone quarried at Nesscliff, 4 miles up the road to the north. He had been appointed County Surveyor of Shropshire in 1787, and this was his first important work. In 1831, when the Denbighshire colliers threatened to march on Shrewsbury to release some of their comrades imprisoned for rioting, the bridge was garrisoned by a squadron of 40 armed pensioners.

96. The Menai Bridge, built by Telford in 1819–26 and still standing nearly a century and a half later. The form of the bridge was virtually imposed on the designer by the requirement of the Admiralty and Trinity House that it should be high enough to avoid all obstruction to shipping. The limestone was brought by coastal vessels from the Penmon quarries, 8 miles east along the Anglesey shore. The chains were forged at Upton Magna in Shropshire, tested at Shrewsbury, dispatched by canal to Chester, and thence shipped to the site by sea. The photograph shows the bridge in its original form, before the extensive reconstruction of 1938–40. All Telford's ironwork was then replaced, and the 16 great chains reduced in number to 4. The masonry of the bridge, however, remains unaltered, and the elegant familiar outline is still as it was when Telford completed the work. The bridge was freed from tolls in 1940.

97. Bonar Bridge, looking from Ross-shire into Sutherland. Telford was appointed engineer to the Commission for Highland Roads and Bridges in 1803, and in the course of the next 20 years he was responsible for a great programme of building. It involved the making of 920 miles of new roads and the reconstruction of 280 miles of older military roads, to render them serviceable to normal civilian traffic. The number of bridges built, reckoning everything from culverts across streams to the great seven-arched bridge over the Tay at Dunkeld, ran to more than 1,000. Nearly all these bridges are still standing. Two of them, that at Craigellachie and this one, had main spans of cast iron 150 ft. wide. Telford intended to use two such spans for Bonar Bridge, but difficulties over foundations led him to modify the design, substituting masonry for the southern half of the bridge. The work dates from 1811–12.

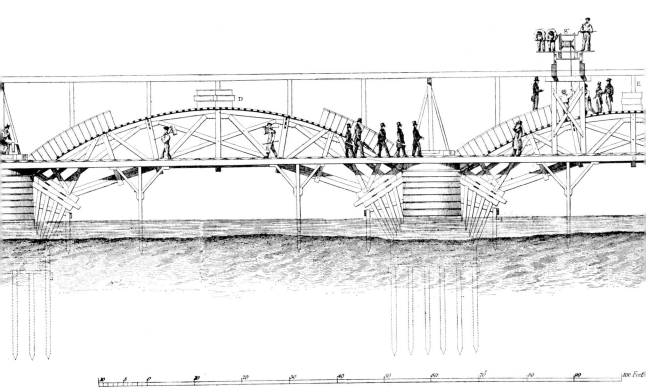

98. The Hutcheson Bridge, Glasgow, under construction. The bridge was built to the design of Robert Stevenson in 1829–33. It was a striking work of municipal improvement, designed to open up the property of Hutcheson's Hospital in the Gorbals, on the south bank of the Clyde; a new road ran south from it to join the turnpike road from Glasgow into Ayrshire. It was replaced by the present Albert Bridge. The original bridge comprised five arches, three of which are shown here. On the left a party of inspection is being received by a foreman or assistant engineer. Dressed stone blocks are being delivered by a railway (built out on a small service bridge), to be raised by windlasses for placing in position. The right-hand arch has been completed, though the timber centering has not yet been removed.

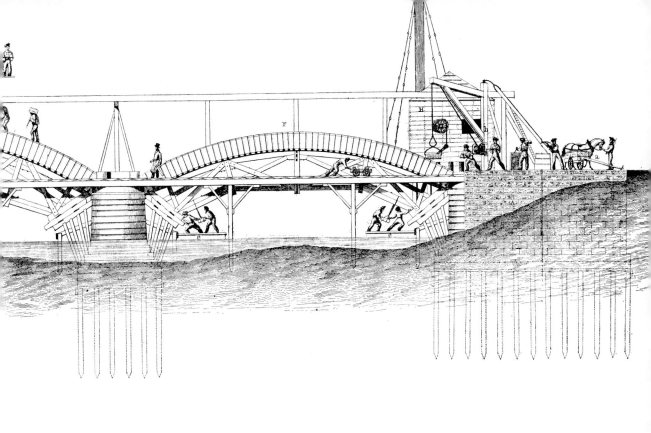

9. Telford's bridge at Bettws-y-Coed on the Holyhead road: justly described by Mr L. T. C. Rolt as 'an extravagant masterpiece of the ironfounder's art', with the rose, thistle, shamrock, and leek in the spandrels. The bridge still stands unaltered.

100. The terminus of the Grand Junction Canal at Paddington Basin, opened in 1801. A passenger boat is departing from the opposite bank.

101. Relief on the mural monument to Joseph Priestley (1743–1817) in the north aisle of Bradford Cathedral. Priestley was Superintendent of the Leeds & Liverpool Canal for nearly 50 years, and this monument was erected at the expense of the company's shareholders as a tribute to his memory. The relief depicts the canal with barges on it and apparently the cutting of a tunnel on the right. It is traditional that the standing figure in the tunnel mouth represents Priestley himself, and that the scene is near Barnoldswick. If so, it must represent the Fenbridge Tunnel with Blacko Tower in the distance

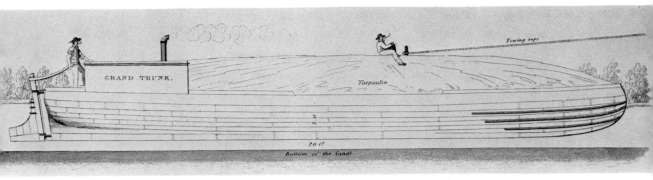

102. Canal boat of the type used on the Birmingham and the Trent & Mersey (or Grand Trunk) Canals: 70 ft. long, 7 ft. 6 in. broad. This print was published in 1838.

103. The *Duchess Countess*, the last example that survived of a canal passenger boat. She was in service on the Bridgewater Canal between Warrington and Manchester (her name recalling that the Duchess of Bridgewater was also Countess of Ellesmere), and when passengers were no longer carried she was sunk. Subsequently raised, she served as a houseboat. She is seen here drawn up out of the water by the Shropshire Union Canal near Frankton.

104. The Trent near Burton Joyce, Notts., by Peter de Wint (1784–1849). The river runs in its natural channels, but a good towing-path has been made for hauling barges that are not propelled by sails.

105. The Kennet & Avon Canal near Newbury. This painting by John Linnell (1792–1882) depicts the canal with minute care, including one of its light timber drawbridges. Notice that the boat in the background is being hauled, or at least manœuvred, by man-power.

106.
The Exeter Custom House of 1681 – so far as is known, the first building to be constructed of brick in the city. The eighteenth-century Harbourmaster's Office, with its curved gable, adjoins it. When the Custom House was built, Exeter ranked high in importance among English ports. London stood first, by a long way, and Bristol second; Exeter disputed with Hull for third place. It maintained this position until about 1715 and then fell back, chiefly through the decline of the Devonshire woollen industry. Today the Quay, and the distinguished buildings on it, are all that is left to remind us of Exeter's former maritime importance.

107.
The Custom House of Lancaster was built in 1764, to the plans of Richard Gillow: a sign of the prosperity and commercial importance of the town in the second half of the eighteenth century – followed by a theatre in 1781, a new Town Hall two years later, and the rebuilding of the bridge in 1788. Lancaster had then a substantial trade with America and the West Indies and was served extensively by coastal shipping. In the nineteenth century it lost this commerce, primarily to Liverpool though also in a smaller degree to Preston, which did much to improve the navigation of the Ribble and opened a dock in 1892.

108. Trinity House, in Trinity Square, just north of the Tower of London. The headquarters of the Brotherhood of Trinity House, which is responsible for the maintenance of sea-marks round the coasts of England and Wales. The building is shown as completed by Samuel Wyatt in 1794. It was heavily damaged in the Second World War and has now been entirely rebuilt to the designs of Sir Albert Richardson. This façade on to Trinity Square has been retained, with the addition of a library on the right-hand side. The restored building was reopened in 1953.

109.
The entrance to Sunderland harbour, with its two lighthouses. The nearer of the two, built largely of timber, stood on the South Pier, and authority was first given for its erection in 1669. It was evidently added to piecemeal in the course of the subsequent century. Its crude timber construction contrasts strongly with that of the trim stone lighthouse on the North Pier, erected in 1803.

110.
The opening of the new Eddystone Lighthouse by the Duke of Edinburgh, 18 May 1882. This was the fourth lighthouse on the site, replacing that completed under Smeaton's direction in 1759. The lower part of Smeaton's building, shown in the picture to the right of the new one, was preserved, the upper part re-erected on Plymouth Hoe. The lighthouse of 1882 threw its beam $17\frac{1}{2}$ miles, compared to the 13 of Smeaton's.

111. Stornoway, *c.* 1815. The town was founded in the reign of James VI, and at the time when this drawing was made its trade was growing rapidly. In 1780 it boasted 15 ships; 40 years later the number had become 74. The fisheries have always been the staple of its business, but the harbour was also much used by Baltic traders; it had accommodated as many as 130 ships at once. The tall building in the foreground covered a fresh-water spring used for supplying ships. Today, with a population of 5,000, Stornoway is the largest town in Ross-shire, and its steamers from Kyle of Lochalsh and air service from Glasgow make it one of the most important centres of communications in the Hebrides.

112. Milford Haven: a new town established by Sir William Hamilton under an Act of 1790. Its early development was due largely to the efforts of Quakers from Nantucket Island, Massachusetts, who were anxious to leave the new United States, and of a French *émigré*, Jean-Louis Barallier. Nelson visited the new town with Sir William and Lady Hamilton in 1801 and described the Haven as, with Trincomalee in Ceylon, the finest harbour he had ever seen. By 1809 there were about 150 houses; a chapel, and an hotel for the use of travellers by the packet-boats to and from Ireland; a custom house, a quay, and a dockyard in which three warships had already been launched. The town is shown here, in an engraving dated 1813, in approximately that condition. By 1831 its population was nearly 2,500. It suffered from the rivalry of other settlements on the Haven, notably Pembroke Dock and Neyland, which became the terminus of the main line of the South Wales Railway in 1856. When steamships were used on the Irish packet service in 1824, they were unable to tie up to the quay; the service was removed to Pembroke Dock in 1836 and to Neyland when the railway opened.

3, Two eighteenth-century Cornish ports. *Above*, the harbour of Portreath on the north coast; begun in
4. 1760 and developed by the Basset family in conjunction with their copper mines inland. Through it
copper ore was exported to Wales, and coal, lime, and other materials needed for the mines were
brought in. The first railway in Cornwall was begun in 1809 to link the mines with Portreath. During
the War of American Independence two small batteries of guns were erected, one on each side of the
harbour, as a defence against privateers. *Below*, the harbour of Charlestown, in the parish of St.
Austell. It owes its establishment to Charles Rashleigh, after whom it was named. He built the first
pier there in 1791, the harbour being cut out of the solid rock. In the early nineteenth century it was
the chief port for the dispatch of the china-clay that was dug a few miles inland, and it developed
a foundry, a ropewalk, and a small shipyard. Though eclipsed now by Fowey (an ancient port, revived
by the china-clay trade) and by Par, Charlestown is still active, as this recent photograph shows.

115. The launch of H.M.S. *Clarence*, 74 guns, at Blackburn's dockyard in Turnchapel, east of Plymouth, 11 April 1812. Then as now, a launch was a social occasion.

117. With the improvement of land communications in the eighteenth and nineteenth centuries the importance of the Long Ferry between London and Gravesend ⟨24–5⟩ declined; but the development of the steamship turned Gravesend for a time into a flourishing pleasure resort. 'New houses,' we are told in 1844, 'new streets, hotels, reading-rooms, public baths, and pleasure gardens have all appeared in succession since the introduction of steam on the river, and now present attractions rarely to be met with in any inland or maritime town of like size. . . . A short sojourn at Gravesend [offers] more animation and variety than is to be met with at any other part of the river.' Here is the scene off Gravesend, with the pier in the distance.

6. An early Clyde steamboat passing Dumbarton. By this date (1813) steamers were plying regularly between Glasgow and Greenock. They normally performed the journey in 3–3½ hours, the same time as that taken by the coach; but with wind and tide in their favour they could sometimes make the passage in 2¼ hours. The funnel was made extremely tall so that it could on occasion serve as a mast and carry sail. The ships were fitted up on the model of the packet-boats on canals. 'The principal cabin for passengers,' we learn, 'is furnished with draught and chess boards, backgammon tables, and other implements of pastime, as well as with a small library of that description of books denominated light reading.' The steamboat was not only (in favourable weather) more comfortable than the coach; it could carry a large number of passengers. One of them was said to have sailed with 247 on board – the complement of nearly a score of coaches.

118, 119. The steamship quickly established itself on the coastal trade between London and Scotland, though passengers were for long divided in their preference for sail or for steam: new sailing ships were being ordered for this traffic as late as 1847. The Dundee, Perth & London Shipping Company (founded by a fusion of two earlier companies in 1826 and one of the oldest shipping firms still in the business today) chartered its first steamer in 1832. It was soon followed by others, including the *Forfarshire* of 270 tons – the largest ship yet built at Dundee. She is seen here (*above*) leaving Hull. In 1838 she was wrecked on the Farne Islands, the survivors of her company being rescued by Grace Darling and her father, keeper of the Longstone lighthouse. Some of the crockery made for use on board the *Forfarshire* is preserved in the Museum at Dundee (*below*).

0. Timber rails for a wagon-way laid in a mine at Groverake, Co. Durham, perhaps about 1815.

1. 'Fish-bellied' iron rails made for the Cromford & High Peak Railway, opened in 1830–1.

122. Wooden bridge over the Tawe near Ystradgynlais (Brecknock), carrying the horse tramroad from the Henrhyd collieries to the Swansea Canal (opened in 1798).

123. The plateway, employing L-shaped rails, was much favoured in some parts of the Midlands and South Wales. This photograph, of a tramroad running from a colliery down to the Derby Canal, shows a primitive type of railway traction still in use unchanged at the end of the nineteenth century. Under the terms of its Act of incorporation (1793) the Derby Canal was obliged to carry, free from toll, up to 5,000 tons of coal a year to Derby for consumption by the poor.

4. Edward Pease (1767–1858) was the son of a Quaker woollen manufacturer of Darlington. He interested himself in the promotion of a railway between Darlington and Stockton in 1818 and three years later, through a meeting with George Stephenson, he was converted to the advantages of steam over horse traction. Thenceforward Pease backed Stephenson steadily and powerfully, advancing him money to start a locomotive works at Newcastle. Without the influence and financial help of Pease, Stephenson's career, and with it the locomotive, would certainly have developed more slowly. Edward Pease was the founder of a strong and wealthy dynasty of men who promoted railways and harbour works, owned coal mines and did much to develop the economic life of Co. Durham.

125. Water-colour sketch by John Dobbin of the opening of the Stockton & Darlington Railway, 27 September 1825. The train is hauled by the engine *Locomotion* and preceded by a horse. All the passengers are travelling in coal wagons except those in the company's one coach *Experiment*. This sketch was subsequently worked up by Dobbin's son into a more famous finished version.

126. This crude engraving gives a good impression of the formidable nature of the Olive Mount cutting on the descent into Liverpool by the Liverpool & Manchester Railway (opened in 1830). Note the position of the guards and the luggage on the roofs of the carriages.

127. The Sankey Viaduct, carrying the Liverpool & Manchester Railway over the first modern canal in Britain, the Sankey Navigation (cf. p. 33). The roughness of construction in the lock and its equipment are well shown here.

28. This engraving of the Leeds & Selby Railway (opened in 1834) gives a good idea of the great changes that railways wrought in the landscape and of the reasons that landowners often had for disliking them. The undulating country visible from the upper windows of the neat gentleman's house on the left has been cut across by the harsh line of the embankment, the railway then slicing its way relentlessly through the opposite hill.

29. *Below.* The construction of Weybridge cutting (1837–8) on the London & Southampton Railway. The brick bridge in front is complete; the earth and rock in the cutting are being removed up the planks on the left of the picture.

30. The 40-arch viaduct at Digswell, near Welwyn, Herts., completed in 1850 to the designs of Lewis Cubitt. The print gives a good idea of the way in which these great works could settle into the landscape and enrich it.

131, 132, 133.

The Crumlin Viaduct, one of the triumphs of iron railway engineering, carrying the line from Ponty-pool to Quakers Yard across Ebbw Vale at a maximum height of 200 ft. It was begun in 1853 and opened in 1857. *Above*, the viaduct when new; *below*, as it is today, with a view of the braced construction of one of the piers.

134. Coal drops at Wallsend, Northumberland. The staith, or wooden pier, bearing the railway from the colliery projects out into deep water. The drop comprises a timber frame hung on pulleys and holding the wagon, which is lowered by gravity into the hatchway of the collier. A man goes down with it who unfastens the bottom of the wagon and so lets the coal fall into the ship's hold. Small ships could be loaded directly from the 'spout', which projects downwards at an angle of 45 degrees through the staith. These drops were invented by William Chapman of Newcastle, *c.* 1800.

135. Though this engraving is dominated by the crane in the foreground, its most remarkable feature is in the middle distance: a very rare representation of the haulage of a passenger train by means of a stationary engine. The scene is at Pittington on the Durham & Sunderland Railway, on which at this time (1844) the whole of the traffic was hauled by this means. The great wheels, with their cables, can be seen beside the engine-house.

136. *Wylam Dilly*, the second oldest locomotive surviving in the world (1814): now in the Royal Scottish Museum, Edinburgh. The oldest, *Puffing Billy* (in the Science Museum, South Kensington), is a year its senior. Both were built under the direction of William Hedley, 'viewer' of Wylam Colliery, Northumberland.

138. One of the first series of Gooch's broad-gauge express engines for the Great Western Railway: *Hirondelle*, completed at Swindon in 1848 and withdrawn from service in 1873 having run 605,000 miles. Notice that the very minimum of protection is provided for the men on the footplate: nothing but a low screen in front, with spectacle glasses and a pair of small side-sheets. At the back of the tender is a seat for the guard to enable him to keep his eye on the whole train.

137. This beautifully-constructed model is an interesting monument of the early history of locomotive engineering in Britain. It was made in 1840, from drawings by Robert Stephenson & Co, by Michael Longridge at Bedlington Works, Northumberland, for presentation to J. D. Forbes, Professor of Natural Philosophy in the University of Edinburgh, by four members of the Longridge family who had been his pupils and friends. No locomotive engineer of that time would have owed a similar debt to any professor in an English university. Edinburgh and Glasgow were the first universities in Britain to take effective notice of the problems of applied science.

139. Goods depot of the Glasgow & Garnkirk Railway (1831). The depot is equipped to deal with all kinds of small traffic, from the miscellaneous small merchandise in the foreground to the coal that is being tipped from staiths into the holds of the colliers on the right.

140. Great Western Railway goods station at Bristol, 1842. The station was built at right angles to the line into the passenger station and 12 ft. below it. (A passenger train can be seen on the embankment to the left.) This arrangement enabled the goods to be moved on a level to and from ships in the Floating Harbour; a special dock was constructed to facilitate trans-shipment and used until 1873. The drawback to the plan was that all vehicles had to be raised and lowered, one by one, to and from the level of the main line. For this purpose a hydraulic lift was provided (seen through the middle archway at the far end of the building, with a covered wagon on it).

41, The Great Northern Railway's terminus at King's Cross, opened in 1852, included not only a splendid
42. station for passengers but also unusually complete provision for the handling of freight. The goods
station was built by the Regent's Canal, and there was a loading dock for barges inside. The building
was generously lighted, both through its glass roof and by lamps; lavishly equipped with cranes; and
sensibly planned to afford the easiest possible interchange between road, canal, and railway. It was
an outstanding example of transport co-ordination in the 1850s.

143. Carriage built for Queen Adelaide by the London & Birmingham Railway in 1842 and preserved today by the British Transport Commission. In its centre compartment the seat could be put into a reclining position, and the vehicle may therefore claim to be a very early ancestor of the sleeping car. Notice how closely the design of the curved side panels reflects that of the mail coaches ⟨76-7⟩.

144. Redhill station, 1865. A type of layout much favoured in the mid-Victorian period, providing complete cover for stopping trains and their passengers and through running roads (for the London-Brighton expresses) in the middle. The iron framework encloses a simple wooden set of waiting-rooms on the left-hand platform.

45. The royal family leaves for Scotland by the Great Northern Railway in 1852. The Queen first travelled by train in 1842 and immediately liked the experience, though she was easily alarmed at speed.

46. The Queen passes under a triumphal arch on the same journey, to the loyal plaudits of a group of onlookers. Royal journeys by train afforded an excellent opportunity of displaying the sovereign to the people, and did something to revive the popular tradition of the monarchy.

147. Interior of first-class railway carriage of the 1840s. The upholstery, the head-rests and arm-rests, the window-straps, are all of the pattern that remained standard for some 80 years.

148. 'To Brighton and back for 3s. 6d.' The excursion train is well rendered in this picture by Charles Rossiter, dated 1859.

CHEAP TRIP TO HULL

ON EASTER TUESDAY, APRIL 2nd, 1872.

THE COMMITTEE OF THE SCARBOROUGH

WORKING MEN'S TEMPERANCE SOCIETY

Respectfully announce that they have arranged with the North Eastern Railway Company to run a Grand

EXCURSION TRAIN

TO THE POPULOUS TOWN OF

HULL

FROM

Scarborough, Filey, & Burlington,

ON EASTER TUESDAY, APRIL 2nd, 1872.

Recreation is necessary to the comfort and happiness of the people. Temperance Societies seek to promote healthy amusements as well as sobriety; and surely there cannot be a more agreeable mode of spending the Holidays---at Easter especially---than having an Excursion to some neighbouring town for a short relaxation from the cares and anxieties of business.

Pleasure Parties will be amply repaid, for there is something attractive at almost every turn. A ramble round the spacious Docks, Wharfs, Quays, and Steamboat Jetties, is worth a visit; these are probably the largest in the Kingdom. In the Market Place, near the South End, stands the noble equestrian gilded Statue of William III, erected in 1735. At the entrance of Junction Street is an elegant Doric Column, upwards of 72 feet in height, erected at a cost of £1,250, and known as the Wilberforce Monument, being a tribute to that great statesman and philanthropist, who was a native of Hull, and whose Statue surmounts the pillar. The Public Buildings in the town are numerous and elegant, to describe which would occupy considerably more space than the limits of this bill will allow.

Leave SCARBRO' at 7 a.m.; FILEY at 7-20 a.m.; BURLINGTON at 8 a.m.

FARES TO HULL AND BACK (COVERED CARRIAGES):

Scarborough and Filey, 2s. 6d.; Burlington, 1s. 6d.

CHILDREN UNDER TWELVE YEARS OF AGE, HALF-PRICE.

THE TRAIN WILL RETURN FROM HULL AT 5 P.M. NO LUGGAGE ALLOWED.

To prevent confusion and facilitate the departure of the train the Booking Offices at Scarborough, Filey, and Bridlington Railway Stations will be open on Saturday, March 30th, from 6-30 to 8 p.m., for the sale of Tickets; and on the morning of April 2nd, previous to departure of the train.

W. W. COOPLAND, PRINTER, SCARBORO'.

149. Excursion handbill, 1872. The train shown is some 30 years out of date. The alternative spellings 'Burlington' and 'Bridlington' are both employed on the bill.

150. Goldsworthy Gurney's steam carriage, which plied between London and Bath in 1833. It carried 60 gallons of water in a shallow, flat tank underneath the body of the vehicle. The engine drove the rear axle. Though the carriage had great potentialities, it did not succeed. Its speed was less than that of the horse-drawn coach; and its weight – 2 tons, concentrated largely on the back axle – punished the roads severely. The turnpike trusts were declared enemies of this coach and of its fellows, and their influence did much to drive them off the roads.

151. Three of the steam buses built by Walter Hancock of Stratford, Essex. Though shown here in a rural landscape, their work was done in London, competing with the horse buses between Paddington and the City in 1833–6. Mechanically, they were not unsuccessful; but, like the long-distance steam coaches, they were hated by the turnpike trusts.

52. The steam carriages were subject to frequent accidents, such as this which befell one on the Paisley road out of Glasgow in 1834. The print demonstrates very clearly the fragile construction of the body of the carriage.

153.
The London cab and its driver as depicted by George Cruikshank in an illustration to *Sketches by Boz* (1839). 'The red cab . . . was omnipresent. You had but to walk down Holborn, or Fleet Street, or any of the principal thoroughfares in which there is a great deal of traffic, and judge for yourself. You had hardly turned into the street, when you saw a trunk or two, lying on the ground: an uprooted post, a hat-box, a portmanteau, and a carpet-bag, strewed about in a very picturesque manner: a horse in a cab standing by, looking about him with great uncon-cern; and a crowd, shouting and scream-ing with delight, cooling their flushed faces against the glass windows of a chemist's shop– "What's the matter here, can you tell me?" – "O'ny a cab, sir."—"Anybody hurt, do you know?" – "On'y the fare, sir. I see him a turnin' the corner, and I ses to another gen'lm'n 'That's a reg'lar little 'oss that, and he's a- comin' along rayther sweet, an't he?' – 'He just is,' ses the other gen'lm'n, ven bump they cums agin the post, and out flies the fare like bricks." Need we say it was the red cab; or that the gentleman with the straw in his mouth who emerged so coolly from the chemist's shop and philosophically climbing into the little dickey, started off at full gallop, was the red cab's licensed driver?'

154. The passing of the mail coach caused deep regret in England. Here James Pollard, who had delineated it so admirably in his prints ⟨75⟩, sketches the entry of the last mail coach into Newcastle on 5 July 1847. Coachman, guard, passengers, and out-riders all wear hatbands of mourning crape, and the coach carries a Union Jack at half-mast. In the background a Tyne steamboat puffs away in sardonic contentment.

155, 156. The supreme elegance of the private horse-carriage. *Above*, coach built by Barker for James Scarlett, 1st Lord Abinger, *c.* 1830. *Below*, Belgrave Square, sketched by the Frenchman Eugène Lami in the 1850s. A pedlar displays his wares on the right; on the left a poor woman and her children watch the lady's glittering departure.

7. Sir Marc Isambard Brunel (1769–1849) was a Frenchman, born near Gisors in Normandy. As a royalist he decided to leave France during the Revolution and emigrated to the United States in 1793. Here he worked as an engineer and architect, designing among other things a theatre in New York. He crossed to England in 1799 and was soon employed by the British Government in designing machinery for use in the dockyards at Portsmouth and Chatham. He was interested in the development of steam navigation, in bridge-building, and in numerous mechanical contrivances. In 1826 he was responsible for the floating landing-piers at Liverpool, of the kind that have been in use there ever since. His plans for a tunnel under the Thames from Wapping to Rotherhithe were taken up by a company formed in 1824, though formidable technical difficulties prevented the completion of the task until 1843. The painter has here shown Brunel with the Thames Tunnel receding behind him and a group of models, symbolising his widespread interest as an engineer and inventor, on the table at his side.

158. The Great Fire of London and other spectacular conflagrations like that at Northampton in 1675 stimulated the development of fire-fighting apparatus. The parish engines were small, crude, and inefficient, and the main burden of fire-fighting came to be assumed by the insurance companies in the eighteenth century. They were keen rivals, each anxious to snatch business from its fellows, and their rivalry was always displayed on the occasion of a great fire, when each company's men would tear through the streets determined to arrive before the rest. The furious speed maintained by the engines and the resplendent uniforms provided for the firemen were a potent form of advertisement. Here is a print by James Pollard, *c.* 1820, showing rival engines converging on a fire.

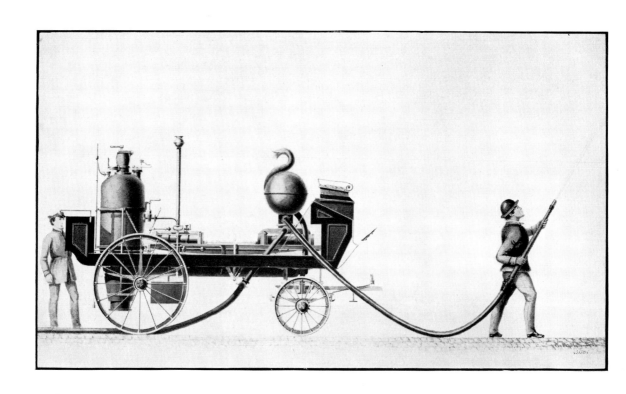

60. The steam traction engine began to make its way in the late 1850s. This machine was built by Tuxford & Sons of Boston, Lincs., in 1857. Similar engines were exported to Cuba for work on sugar plantations. They were equipped with the 'endless railway' patented by James Boydell in 1846 and 1854: a series of shoes overlapping one another to form a continuous track. This engine weighed 12 tons and was sold at £1,020.

59. The first steam fire engine constructed in England (1830). It was designed by Braithwaite and ◀ Ericsson, and by steam power it was able to project 40 tons of water an hour up to a height of 90 ft. Its haulage was still performed by horses. Drawing of 1869, certified by Braithwaite.

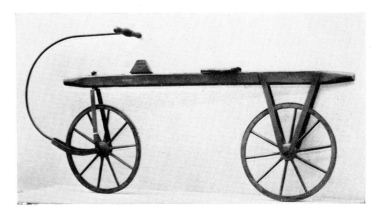

161.

The earliest ancestors of the bicycle appeared experimentally in the eighteenth century. The 'hobby horse' or 'dandy horse' became a momentary craze in Revolutionary Paris, and in an improved form it was introduced into Britain in about 1818. This is an early British example. The rider propelled himself forward by striking his feet alternately on the ground.

162.

The bicycle emancipated itself from the hobby-horse first in Scotland. In 1839 Kirkpatrick MacMillan, a young blacksmith of Courthill in Dumfriesshire, built a machine whose rider propelled it by treadles, without touching the ground. Though this historic bicycle has itself disappeared, one or two copies of it made in Scotland survive. Perhaps the earliest is this one, built about 1842 by Gavin Dalzel of Lesmahagow, Lanarkshire.

163.

Although the invention of the bicycle may fairly be attributed to MacMillan, the use of pedals, and the manufacture of bicycles on a substantial scale, was developed in France by the brothers Michaux in the 1860s. In Britain the manufacture came to be centred on Coventry, largely for an accidental reason. A young man named Rowley Turner, nephew of the manager of the Coventry Sewing Machine Company and its agent in Paris, became interested in the Michaux bicycles. At a time of slack trade in sewing machines he persuaded the company through his uncle to experiment with the production of bicycles for the French market. The outbreak of the Franco-Prussian War in 1870, however, cut off this market for the time being, and the Coventry firm turned to the home market instead. Though the bicycle illustrated is not one of Turner's, it is a somewhat heavier contemporary version of the same kind of machine, universally known – with good reason – as the 'boneshaker'. It was built by K. F. Hedges at the Erith Ironworks in 1869.

164.

The 'ordinary' bicycle (or 'penny-farthing') represented an improvement on the boneshaker. Though the art of riding it was more difficult to acquire, it was a much lighter machine. This Bayliss-Thomas bicycle of 1879 weighed 49 lb. against the 68 lb. of the Hedges machine; a racing version was produced in the eighties weighing only $21\frac{1}{2}$ lb.

165.

Socially, cycling was not only a poor man's pastime. The National Cyclists' Union owed a great deal to Viscount Bury (later 7th Earl of Albemarle), who was its President from 1883 to his death in 1894. He is seen here on his tricycle.

166.

The 'safety' bicycle established itself in the 1880s, and by the following decade it entirely displaced the 'ordinary'. It took its name from the increased safety that was offered to the rider by the lowering of the saddle, and this alteration became practicable with the development of the chain drive on the rear axle. This and the diamond frame produced, in essence, the bicycle we know today. Here is an early example, recognisably of the modern type: a Singer machine of about 1890. It is fitted with solid tyres; but J. B. Dunlop had already patented a pneumatic tyre for bicycles, and by 1895 this pattern had superseded the solid tyre altogether.

167.

Although the idea of the power-driven bicycle made its appearance in a shadowy form early in the nineteenth century, it was not until the 1880s that it began to attract much serious attention, and then notably in Germany and England. Its evolution from the early crude and fantastic designs was rapid, and by the first decade of the twentieth century it had come to embrace most of the essential features of the machine we know today. This is a Singer motorcycle of 1903, with the power unit mounted on the rear wheel.

168.

The Triumph Junior motor-cycle of 1914: one of the most successful of the designs produced before and during the First World War. The engine developed $2\frac{1}{4}$ h.p., and the whole machine turned the scale at the moderate weight of 130 lb.

59. The American G. F. Train established three experimental lines of tramway in London in 1861, in Bayswater, in Victoria St., and from the south side of Westminster Bridge to Kennington Gate. This is the car running on the second of these routes. Though the print is damaged it is of great interest as the earliest surviving photograph of a London tram. The services were short-lived, the last of them disappearing in June 1862. Train also established tramways at Birkenhead, at Darlington, and in the Potteries; the first and third of these enjoyed a long life.

70. Horse-trams began to run in Leicester in 1874. Here is one at the Groby Road terminus, on the west of the town, in 1902. Electric traction began two years later.

171. Horse-tram of the North Metropolitan Company plying between Holborn Town Hall and Stamford Hill *c.* 1890. Note the 'knife-board' back-to-back seats on the roof.

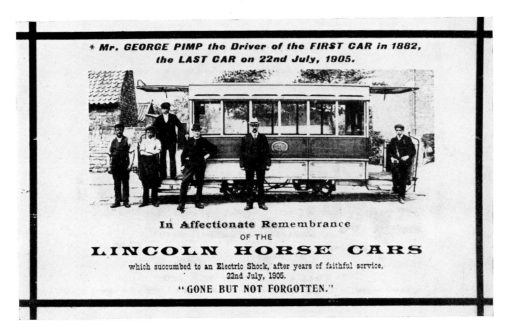

172. Just as the passing of the stage-coach was deeply regretted by the romantically-minded ⟨154⟩, so the horse tram was mourned when it was ousted by its electrically-operated successors. This card was produced to commemorate the demise of horse trams in Lincoln.

75. Thomas Tilling set his first horse-bus plying between Peckham and Oxford Circus when the Great Exhibition was being held in Hyde Park in 1851. The business that he founded grew steadily, until more than 1,000 horses were employed in it. Here is one of his buses running between Putney and Battersea in the last years of the nineteenth century. Note the range of the firm's activities and the number of its branches, enumerated on the side of the bus.

73. The character of the horse tram driver (t) has been well caught in this photograph. His left hand holds the reins, his right the brake, and he is heavily armoured in leather.

74. Side by side with him we may put Joe (t) Green (or 'Sand Joe', as he was usually called), as the type of the street tradesman of the late nineteenth century, selling sand in Bradford from his horse-drawn cart. He forms one of a remarkable gallery of 'Bradford Street Characters' drawn by J. Sowden.

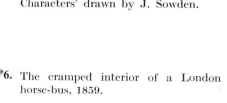

76. The cramped interior of a London horse-bus, 1859.

G

177. Fleet Street and Ludgate Hill at the end of the nineteenth century. Traffic congestion was already a serious problem, and almost immediately afterwards it began to be aggravated by the spread of the motor vehicle, moving at a different speed from the horse.

179. Tower Bridge under construction, April 1892. The bridge was designed to open in order to allow the passage of large ships into and out of the upper part of the Pool of London. It was completed in 1894. The hydraulic machinery was encased in the steel-framed towers, shown here before they had received their stone casing with its Gothic decoration. The bridge has become a familiar part of the London scene, but as Prof. Pevsner rightly remarks it 'does much damage to the skyline of the City, and the apparent scale of the Tower'.

178. Battersea Bridge, by Walter Greaves (1874). Until 1773 the Thames could be crossed at this point only by a ferry. In that year a timber bridge was completed, mainly at the charge of Earl Spencer, who was lord of the manor of Battersea. In 1873 the bridge was acquired by the Albert Bridge Company and improved for navigation by the widening of two arches, the structure being strengthened at the same time by iron girders and additional piles. The bridge lasted in this condition, portrayed here, only for a short time. In 1885–6 it was demolished and replaced by the present iron structure. The sails of the barge and the funnel of the steamer are both lowered for the passage of the bridge. The Crystal Palace is visible on the skyline at the right-hand side of the picture. Greaves was the son of a Chelsea waterman and boatbuilder, and just as his father used to row Turner on the Thames, so Walter and his brother Harry used to row Whistler. His rendering of the scene has an especially literal fidelity to truth: he painted the river and its craft with intimate knowledge.

180. The idea of bridging the Firth of Forth at or near the Queen's Ferry is an old one. James Anderson, for example, proposed a suspension bridge in 1818, along almost exactly the same route as the present railway bridge. In 1873 a Forth Bridge Railway Company was formed by the North British and three English railways, and work was begun on a steel suspension bridge to the designs of Thomas Bouch. It had not proceeded far, however, when Bouch's Tay Bridge met with disaster, and the engineer's reputation was destroyed with it. A new plan was then adopted on the cantilever principle, to the designs of Benjamin Baker and Sir John Fowler, and this bridge was at last opened on 4 March 1890. This view is taken from the south, looking over to North Queensferry and Inverkeithing. The Queen's Ferry still conveys passengers and vehicles across from the pier to the left of the bridge.

182. The Newtown & Machynlleth Railway under construction, *c.* 1862. This photograph shows work in progress on the Talerddig cutting, the most difficult engineering work on the line. The cutting runs through solid rock and is 120 ft. deep. Some gold was found during construction. The railway was officially opened on 3 January 1863, when the young Marquess of Blandford rode on one of the engines playing 'See the Conquering Hero Comes' on the cornet-à-piston. The traveller still passes through this cutting today: it is the highest point on the line between Shrewsbury and Aberystwyth.

181. The works of the Channel Tunnel at the west end of Shakespeare Cliff, Dover. Some 2,000 yards of the tunnel were driven here in 1880–2. The work was not proceeded with further, though the scheme for a tunnel on different lines has been revived recently and is still under active discussion.

183. Oxted tunnel, London, Brighton & South Coast Railway; photograph taken in May 1884, showing the drainage channel beside the track arched over in brick but not yet covered in.

184. The station staff at Retford, Great Northern Railway, *c.* 1885. Every one seems to have turned out for the occasion, including a dog and a cart-horse. The locomotive is Patrick Stirling's 2–4–0 no. 265.

185. The locomotive lent itself well to decoration, and much the same care was lavished on it on state occasions as on a cart-horse being dressed for a fair. The London, Brighton & South Coast Railway ran an annual Stationmasters' and Inspectors' Excursion, in aid of a widows' fund maintained by the company; and the engine that hauled the train for that event was appropriately bedizened, to a different pattern every year. This photograph shows a brand-new B2 locomotive, 205 *Henry Fletcher*, in 1897, got up to salute the Diamond Jubilee, with a bust of the queen over the buffers and her portrait in a medallion on the tender. Even the coal has been whitewashed.

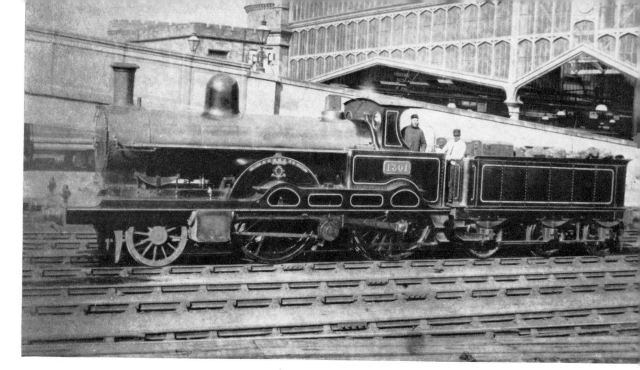

186. F. W. Webb designed five series of compound express engines for the London and North Western Railway. The most successful series was the *Teutonic* class of 1889, one of which, 1306 *Jeanie Deans*, worked the 2 p.m. Scotch express from Euston to Crewe daily for $8\frac{1}{2}$ years. *Teutonic* is seen here at the north end of Carlisle station, probably having just come off the morning Scotch express from London. Notice the great Gothic screen to the roof, which has only very lately been removed.

187. The British express engine at the height of its beauty. One of the D class of 1901 designed by H. S. Wainwright for the South Eastern & Chatham Railway. The engine is shown here as restored for preservation by the British Transport Commission.

188.

The paddle-steamer *Malakoff*, one of four used by Capt. Jackson of New Milford (i.e. Neyland) on the services to Waterford and Cork. In 1871 the Great Western Railway secured Parliamentary powers to work this service, buying Capt. Jackson out and operating the ships itself from 1 February 1872. The *Malakoff* was built by John Scott Russell at Millwall in 1851 and began life as the *Baron Osy*, trading between London and Antwerp. She was transferred to a London registration and acquired her new name during the Crimean War. She remained on the Irish service from 1864 to 1884. She is seen here drawn up out of the water at New Milford. Notice the decorative work on her stern – the tradition of the gallery, going back to the sixteenth century ⟨23⟩ and lasting into the Age of Steam.

189.

Paddle steamer *Eclair* at Ilfracombe about 1870. The *Eclair* (237 tons) was built at Port Glasgow in 1865 and plied on an all-the-year-round service between Cardiff, Belfast, Bideford, and Tenby from 1859 to 1872. From 1876 to 1888 she worked on the Thames.

190.

Paddle steamer *Madge Wildfire*. She was built at Ayr in 1886 and was one of the first ships to be acquired by the Caledonian Steam Packet Co. on its formation in 1888. The company was a subsidiary of the Caledonian Railway, formed to exploit the opening of its line to Gourock in 1889. She was acquired by Buchanan Steamers Ltd. in 1913 and renamed *Isle of Skye*. She was the first steamer to resume sailings between Glasgow and the Clyde ports in 1919. In 1927 she was transferred to the Forth under the name *Fair Maid* and the ownership of the Grangemouth & Forth Trading Co. She survived until the Second World War.

1. The 'water-bus' enjoyed, for a time, great popularity both in Glasgow and in London. In Glasgow the Clyde Trustees secured powers to operate steamers in 1878, and in 1884 they put on a service from the Victoria Bridge, close to St. Enoch station, to Whiteinch, nearly four miles downstream. Four vessels were used, each 74 ft. long and accommodating 235 passengers. They all bore the name *Clutha* (the Celtic form of 'Clyde') and were distinguished from one another only by numbers. The service was always called after the boats. Twelve more *Cluthas* were eventually built down to 1896. The opening of the Glasgow Subway (p. 57) in 1897 damaged their business; the electric trams, which began to run in Glasgow in 1901, destroyed it. The service was abandoned in Nov. 1903. At its height it had carried nearly 3 million passengers a year.

2. The South Eastern & Chatham Railway's steamer *The Queen*, built by Denny of Dumbarton in 1902. She was the first cross-channel steamer to be propelled by turbines, and the first to make the crossing in an hour. She is seen here at the Admiralty Pier at Dover taking passengers on board from a boat train. Note the container that is being swung over by a crane on to the ship from a flat truck next to the engine. *The Queen* became a military transport in the First World War and was sunk in 1916.

193. The building and repair of quite substantial ships continued to be undertaken in very small and remote places as long as the timber sailing ship lasted. Here is a photograph of shipbuilding on the beach at Nevin, Caernarvonshire, in 1880. The vessel in the foreground is the schooner *Venus* (120 tons), the last ship constructed there. At least 118 ships had been built on this beach since 1760.

194. Another picture of Nevin, showing the *Mary Goldsworthy*, a wherry of 48 tons built at Ulverston in 1865, waiting to discharge coal. Much coal continued to be transported by sea, for cheapness, even when the railway system was complete; particularly in districts so remote as this, 8 miles from the railhead at Pwllheli.

95. The paddle steamer *St. George*, on the Liverpool–Douglas service, wrecked on the Conister Rock, Isle of Man, on 20 November 1830. All the 22 people on board were rescued by a new lifeboat, used before it had been tested, under the direction of Sir William Hillary, who had been chiefly responsible for founding the National Institution for the Preservation of Life from Shipwreck (now the Royal National Lifeboat Institution) in 1824. Few Englishmen have been greater benefactors of humanity.

96. Lifeboat and crew, *c.* 1885.

197.

On the Grand Junction Canal at Rickmansworth, *c.* 1900. By the end of the Victorian age, although the great canals still carried a substantial traffic, they had come to be considered picturesque subjects for the landscape painter.

198.

A disused 'flash lock' or 'staunch' on the Little Ouse, near Thetford. The flash lock comprised a weir with a central gate raised vertically to give passage to boats. The church in the background is Santon All Saints, on the Norfolk bank of the river.

199.

In the 1870s and 1880s, as river traffic declined, rowing and punting and camping-out became popular pastimes. Henry Taunt's *New Map of the River Thames* (1872), illustrated with 100 of his photographs and a delightfully avuncular text, gave something of the flavour of these pleasures – as Jerome K. Jerome's *Three Men in a Boat* did, less solemnly, in 1889.

200.

The construction of the Manchester Ship Canal in 1887–93, at a cost of over £14 million, was the greatest work of its kind ever undertaken in Britain. These photographs give some idea of the magnitude of the task. They show (*above*) the cutting near Eastham, the point at which the canal joined the Mersey; and (*below*) the making of the Eastham locks.

201.

202.
This photograph gives a good idea of the conditions of travelling and working on the London Underground in the days of steam. It shows a Hammersmith train at Aldgate shortly before the line was electrified in 1905.

203.
The Central London Railway was opened in 1900. It ran from the Bank to Shepherd's Bush and was known, from its uniform fare, as the Twopenny Tube. The trains comprised seven coaches, accommodating 336 passengers, hauled by separate electric locomotives. Two of them are seen here in the company's car sheds in 1902.

204.
A group of the original electric locomotives used on the Central London tube. They were replaced by coaches with built-in electric motors in 1902.

205.
The rail motor car had a brief vogue in the early years of the twentieth century. Introduced in its modern form on to the London & South Western Railway in 1903, it comprised a combined locomotive and coach. It was economical to build and flexible in operation, since it could be driven from either end; it was the railways' answer to the electric tram and the motor bus. Here is a rail motor built for the Taff Vale Railway standing outside the Brush Works, Loughborough, where it was made.

6. A drawing-room car built by the South Eastern Railway in 1897 for service between London and Folkestone. The curves of its ironwork, the loops of its curtains, and the tassels of its chairs all reflect accurately the middle-class taste of the end of the century.

7. The buffet car *Mary Seaton*, built by the Pullman Car Company for service on the Caledonian Railway in 1914. With its decoration after (a very long way after) Adam and its solid leather armchairs, it is clearly designed to suggest a London club-room.

208.

Electrification of the trams at Portsmouth, 1902. The process involved much disturbance of streets, both in putting up standards and in laying the track. Even where horse tramways were already in operation, it was frequently necessary to re-lay the system completely to enable the track to withstand the heavier loads placed on it by the larger electric tramcars.

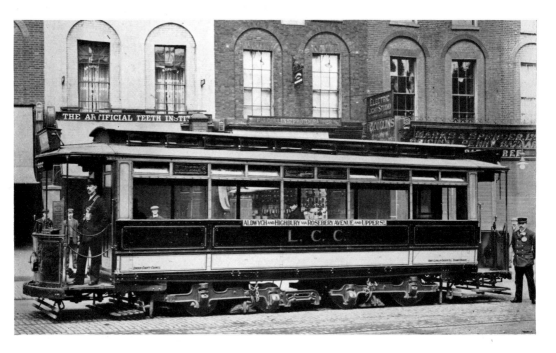

210.

The trolley-bus derives from the work of Werner von Siemens in Berlin from 1882 onwards. It was first demonstrated in this country by the Railless Electric Traction Company, which put this experimental car through its paces at the Colindale depot of the Metropolitan Electric Tramways in September 1909. The destination board is misleading, for the vehicle never ran on the route indicated.

1. Three-wheeled steam wagonette built by Catley & Ayres of York in 1868. It was used for some three years. The makers claimed that it would run at 20 m.p.h. on a good road; but the British legislation of the period (see p. 60) prevented it and other similar vehicles from showing their full capabilities. One of the very few surviving steam carriages of the sixties or seventies is the Grenville carriage of 1875, now in Bristol City Museum.

9. Single-deck L.C.C. electric tram, designed for running through the Kingsway tunnel. The northern section of the tunnel, from Aldwych to Holborn, was opened in 1906. This photograph was probably taken between November 1906, when the service was extended to Highbury, and April 1908, when the tunnel was completed to the Embankment.

2. Peberdy motor car at Cossington, Leicestershire, 1897.

213. The first English Daimler motor-car, built at Coventry in 1897. It was a 2-cylinder machine, developing 4 h.p.

214.

An attempt to adapt the traditional form of the hansom cab to motor traction (1906). The body was mounted on a standard Vauxhall chassis, with the controls arranged so that the driver operated them from aloft at the back.

215.

The Vauxhall Ironworks began to produce cars in 1903. This is no. 6, built in that year: a 5 h.p. machine with a single-cylinder water-cooled engine, designed to attain a maximum speed of 25 m.p.h. In 1956 this car was driven from London to Brighton in 3¾ hours.

216

The motor charabanc came into its own in the reign of Edward VII. Two Fiat vehicles are being used here for the annual outing of the church Bible class from Kirby Moorside, in the North Riding of Yorkshire, on 3 June 1909.

217

With the Silver Ghost of 1907 Rolls-Royce produced the first of a long line of motor-cars that gave the firm's name a unique reputation. It concentrated on producing cars of the highest class, elegant, smooth, noiseless, and completely reliable. They were sought by wealthy and discriminating purchasers from all over the world, as they still are today.

218. The motor-car began to serve political purposes before the outbreak of the First World War. Here a car is being used to convey fish porters to the polls at the Grimsby by-election of 12 May 1914. The cheering crowd in the background gives an indication of the novelty of the event.

219. Something of the elegance of the aristocratic horse-drawn carriage ⟨155-6⟩ survived into the early motoring age. This is a posed photograph, taken just before the First World War, of a car to be hired from the firm of Dawson & Higgins.

0. The B Type was the first reliable motor-bus owned by the London General Omnibus Company. It proved itself in a few months after its introduction in October 1910, and 2,500 of the same design were built within the next three years. 1,300 of these served on the Western Front during the First World War.

1. So successful was the B type that within a year of its introduction the General company withdrew the last of its horse buses. They were then all swiftly broken up, so that today no General horse bus survives, though one belonging to the Star Company, which plied between Camberwell and Clapham, is preserved in the Maidstone Museum of Carriages.

222. The development of motoring on a large scale after the First World War revived the old coaching inns, whose trade had suffered a decline during the Railway Age. Here is the courtyard of the George at Huntingdon in 1925, with its characteristic seventeenth-century wooden gallery. Both the cars in the picture bear Huntingdonshire registration numbers. Long-distance motoring had not yet turned all hotels on the Great North Road into stopping-places on the way to and from London.

223. Traffic congestion in the Strand, at the entrance into Trafalgar Square. The block of buildings in the left foreground was replaced by South Africa House in 1935. The buses are of the NS type of 1923, one of them with a covered top – an innovation dating from 1925.

24. One of the six prototype Austin Seven cars built in 1922: the most famous and successful of all miniature cars in the inter-war period. Between 1923, when the model went into production, and 1938, when it was at last discontinued, 350,000 were built, in addition to others turned out under licence in France, Germany and the U.S.A. The car first sold for £225, but by 1930 its price had gone down to £125. In the advertising catchphrase of the twenties, the Austin Seven claimed to provide 'motoring for the million'. Few such catchphrases have been better justified.

25. A paraffin-engined locomotive hauling a train at a munitions depot in 1915. These locomotives, built by Ruston's of Lincoln, were designed for operation with the greatest possible ease and simplicity. This one is being driven by a woman, and another woman sits by her in the cab: something quite unimaginable before 1914.

226. The up Silver Jubilee express picking up water on Langley troughs, near Stevenage. The Silver Jubilee (introduced in 1935) was the first of a series of high-speed express trains, on which the locomotives and rolling stock were streamlined throughout, introduced by the London & North Eastern Railway. It did the journey between King's Cross and Newcastle in four hours. These trains, together with a similar one operated by the London Midland & Scottish Railway between Euston and Glasgow in 1937–9, represent the crowning achievement of express train working with steam engines in this country.

227. The exterior and interior of the diesel-electric Midland Pullman train, introduced by British Railways and the Pullman Car Company in 1960. The train is air-conditioned and so insulated as to be practically noiseless in motion. It is the British equivalent of the Trans-Europe Express.

228.
Cartoon by Ionicus for *Punch*.

229.
Demolition of a bridge at Rainham in 1957 for the electrification of the Kent Coast railway line. The density of traffic on the British railways makes it possible to undertake such work (which is essential for the completion of the Modernisation Plan of 1955) only on Saturday nights and Sundays. $5\frac{1}{2}$ hours were all that could be allowed for this operation, including the removal of the rubble and the repair of any track or works damaged by inadvertence.

LEEDS—NOTTINGHAM—LONDON—PARIS
(Daily)
L. S. and P.A.

Miles	Airports of		§			Airports of		§	
0	LEEDS ... ...dep	11 20	13 40		PARIS ... ...dep	...	9 30		
65	NOTTINGHAM ... arr	11 50	14 10		HESTON ... ... arr	...	11 25		
"	...dep	12 0	14 20		" ... ...dep	9 30	11 45		
175	HESTON ... ... arr	12 55	15 15		NOTTINGHAM ... arr	10 25	12 40		
"	...dep	13 25	...		" ... ...dep	10 35	12 50		
435	PARIS ... ... arr	15 20	...		LEEDS ... ... arr	11 5	13 20		

§ Lands at Berck (for Le Touquet) by special arrangement

Distance and Time allowance for conveyance between Airport and Town Terminus

TOWN	AIRPORT	TOWN TERMINUS	Miles	Minutes
LEEDS	Sherburn in Elmet	Corn Exchange	12	40
NOTTINGHAM	Tollerton	Black Boy Hotel...	2½	30
LONDON	Heston	Langham Hotel, Portland Place, W. 1...........	14	45
PARIS	Le Bourget	France—Tourisme, 4-6 Rue de Sèze	—	45

FARES

	NOTTINGHAM			LONDON			LE TOUQUET			PARIS		
	Single	Ret.	Ex. Bg.	Single	Ret.	Ex. Bg.	Single	Ret.	Ex. Bg.	Single	Ret.	Ex. Bg.
	s. d.	s. d.	s. d.	s. d.	s. d.	s. d.	s. d.	s. d.	s. d.	s. d.	s. d.	s. d.
LEEDS	18 0	30 0	0 3	42 0	70 0	0 6	84 0	147 0	0 6	105 0	189 0	0 6
NOTTINGH'M	...	...	...	25 0	45 0	0 6	70 0	130 0	0 6	90 0	170 0	0 6

Ex. Bag.—Excess Baggage per lb.

230. A page from the first issue of *Bradshaw's International Air Guide* (November 1934), showing two internal British services. Very few of those then operated have proved permanently profitable. Though there was already a daily service between London and Belfast (in 3½ hours), there was none between London and Edinburgh or Glasgow. The service offered by London Scottish & Provincial Airways Ltd between Leeds, Nottingham and London was promising, but its usefulness was reduced by the remoteness of the airports and the impossibility of providing an adequate out-and-back service in the day for business men, since flying was conducted only during the hours of daylight. To and from Paris, however, it was much quicker than that provided by surface transport.

232. A B.E.A. Heron landing on the beach at Barra. This regular service (daily in summer, four times a week in winter) between Glasgow and a number of points in the Hebrides continues the work begun by Telford and the early paddle steamers to bring the Western Isles into close and constant touch with the mainland of Scotland.

231.

◀ Guernsey & Jersey Airways' D.H. Flamingo flying over Portelet Bay, Jersey, in the summer of 1939.

233. The last tram to run in London arriving at New Cross depot, illuminated by flares and greeted by a great crowd, on the night of 5–6 July 1952.

234. The contemporary traffic problem. The evening rush hour on Putney Bridge, the traffic streaming southwards out of London, 1961.

235. The Dover Stage, opened in 1957. This hotel (architect L. Erde) was designed for the accommodation of coach parties travelling to and from the Continent and was the first of its kind in Europe. The business of Dover has recently boomed, owing to the development of coach travel and of the ferries for private cars. In the single month of August 1956, 448,000 passengers passed through the port; in 1960 the corresponding figure was 669,000.

236. The improvement of roads is not confined to the great trunk routes and the urbanised parts of Britain. Here, in the Outer Hebrides, is the new causeway linking the islands of Benbecula and North Uist, opened by the Queen Mother in 1960. Since Benbecula was linked to South Uist by a viaduct in 1943, it is now possible to drive continuously across the three islands. The causeway was built by local men, using 350,000 tons of rock quarried from one of the small islands over which it passes. It will help to develop the islands' tourist trade and their industries, like tweed-making.

237. The construction of the new motorways involves the most considerable upheaval of the landscape since the building of the railways a century ago. Here is the excavation of the cutting through the chalk downs between Luton and Dunstable, to carry M1 from London to Birmingham.

238. This view gives some idea of the new ▶ patterns the motorways will impose upon the landscape of Britain. It shows the elaborate two-tier junction of M1 with A508, the road from Stony Stratford to Northampton, near Collingtree, Northants.

239. This picture covers a span of history from the first century A.D. to the twentieth. It shows the western edge of the old town of Leicester. The settlement first became important early in the Roman occupation of Britain, guarding the point at which the Foss Way crossed the River Soar. The modern successor of the Foss Way runs transversely across the picture from right to left; it crosses the river's two arms by the Bow Bridge (right) and the West Bridge (left centre). The Roman town grew up at the left-hand side of the picture, on rising ground above the West Bridge. The Normans built a castle on a new site, equally well adapted for guarding the river-crossing; the mound and the hall of the building remain (marked with an arrow). In the eighteenth century the left-hand arm of the Soar was rendered navigable, with a towing-path, and factories began to be built along it in consequence. In 1832 the Leicester & Swannington Railway, the first steam-operated railway in the Midlands, was opened, running to a terminus in the foreground of the picture; the buildings have now gone, but some of the tracks are still in use. Sixty years later the Great Central Railway superimposed itself on the old town, striding across it on a continuous viaduct three-quarters of a mile long. The sequence of transport development may be said to be completed by the aircraft from which the photograph was taken. It is not too much to say that the whole industrial complex seen here springs from the transport facilities that have been concentrated in this small area, half a mile deep and a quarter of a mile wide. In itself the photograph epitomises much of the story told in this book.

Notes

1. T. S. Willan, *River Navigation in England, 1600–1750* (1936), 5.

2. For the origins of the coal trade by sea cf. J. U. Nef, *Rise of the British Coal Industry* (1932), i. 9–10; S. Middlebrook, *Newcastle-upon-Tyne* (1950), 41.

3. *V. C. H. Northants.*, ii. 293–5.

4. W. J. Arkell, *Oxford Stone* (1947), 61. Similarly Burford stone was taken to Radcot Bridge, near Faringdon, for shipment in the seventeenth century: *ibid.*, 69.

5. See I. D. Margary, *Roman Ways in the Weald* (1948). The same author's *Roman Roads in Britain* (2 vols., 1955–7) is now the standard work on the subject.

6. See the map in W. G. Hoskins and H. P. R. Finberg, *Devonshire Studies* (1952), opp. p. 225.

7. E. Jervoise, *Ancient Bridges of Wales and Western England* (1936), v. Of the 53 road bridges in Leicestershire (excluding those for railways and canals), more than half are medieval or stand on the site of a medieval predecessor: *V. C. H. Leics.*, iii. 69, 85–90.

8. A good facsimile of the Gough Map was published in 1958 with a useful commentary by E. J. S. Parsons and Sir Frank Stenton.

9. *Accounts of the Lord High Treasurer of Scotland*, vol. iv, pp. li–lviii.

10. E. Carus-Wilson in *Studies in English Trade in the Fifteenth Century*, ed. E. Power and M. M. Postan (1933), 245.

11. R. and R. C. Anderson, *The Sailing Ship* (1926), 115.

12. I am much indebted here to the admirably lucid account of this matter in J. A. Williamson, *The English Channel* (1959), chaps. v and vi.

13. A. Ruddock, *Italian Merchants and Shipping in Southampton, 1270–1600* (1951); *The Brokage Book of Southampton, 1443–44*, ed. O. Coleman, i (1959).

14. J. Townsend, *History of Abingdon* (1910), 52–3; *V. C. H. Berks.*, iii. 522, iv. 435–6. The undertaking at Abingdon was commemorated in a fifteenth-century poem by Richard Forman and in a history of the gild dating from about 1627. Both were printed in 1872 under the title *A Monument of Christian Munificence*, ed. C. D. Cobham.

15. Cf. C. A. J. Armstrong, 'Some Examples of the Distribution and Speed of News in England at the Time of the Wars of the Roses': *Studies in Medieval History presented to F. M. Powicke* (1948), 429–54.

16. *Register of the Privy Council of Scotland*, iii. 121–2, v. 531–2, viii. 599–600; *New Statistical Account of Scotland*, x (1845), 42–3.

17. R. Holinshed, *Chronicles* (1587 ed.), i. 114.

NOTES

18. For a clear illustration of the working of the system, based on the Quarter Sessions records of the North Riding of Yorkshire, see E. Trotter, *Seventeenth Century Life in the Country Parish* (1919), chap. vi.

19. *Kentish Sources: Some Roads and Bridges*, ed. E. Melling (1958), 18.

20. *The Welsh Port Books, 1550–1603*, ed. E. A. Lewis (1927), xxviii–xxix; *Hist. MSS. Comm. De L'Isle and Dudley*, i. 316–21.

21. Nef, *Rise of the British Coal Industry*, i. 21; Middlebrook, *Newcastle-upon-Tyne*, 65; T. S. Willan, *The English Coasting Trade, 1600–1750* (1938), 11–14.

22. Nef, i. 101–3; M. E. Finch, *The Wealth of Five Northamptonshire Families* (1956), 150.

23. J. W. W. Bund, *The Civil War in Worcestershire* (1905), 10, and 'Worcestershire Bridges' in *Reports and Papers of the Associated Architectural Societies*, xxxi (1911–12), 273–302; *Quarter Sessions Records for the County of Somerset* (Somerset Record Society), iii. 6.

24. *Early Travellers in Scotland*, ed. P. Hume Brown (1891); W. B. Rye, *England as seen by Foreigners* (1865); *Thomas Platter's Travels in England*, ed. C. Williams (1937).

25. *A Relation of a Short Survey of 26 Counties*, ed. L. G. W. Legg (1904).

26. E. G. Box in *Archaeologia Cantiana*, xlv (1933), 48–59.

27. *Early Travellers in Scotland*, 162–81.

28. British Museum Lansdowne MS. 170, ff. 269–73.

29. *Works* (1630), part ii, p. 237.

30. *Quarter Sessions Records for Somerset*, iii. 11; *Kentish Sources: Roads and Bridges*, 4.

31. Willan, *River Navigation*, 6.

32. W. T. Jackman, *Development of Transportation in Modern England* (1916), i. 165–8; R. M. Robbins, *Middlesex* (1953), 64, 247; *Hist. MSS. Comm. Salisbury*, iii. 354–5.

33. D. Defoe, *Tour through the whole Island of Great Britain*, ed. G. D. H. Cole (1927), ii. 521.

34. *Ibid.*, ii. 527–8.

35. *V. C. H. Wilts.*, iv. 256–8.

36. W. Marshall, *Rural Economy of the Midland Counties* (1790), i. 37–9, 52n., 81–2.

37. A. Young, *Six Months' Tour through the North of England* (1771), iv. 430.

38. T. Pennant, *Journey from Chester to London* (1782), 138.

39. C. de Saussure, *A Foreign View of England in the Reigns of George I and George II* (1902), 147; F. Kielmansegge, *Diary of a Journey to England* (1902), 17–19, 135–6; F. de St. Fond, *Journey through England and Scotland to the Hebrides in 1784* (1907), i. 124–5, 179, 298–300.

40. H. G. Graham, *Social Life of Scotland in the Eighteenth Century* (1950 ed.), 168. Cf. A. H. Dodd, 'The Roads of North Wales, 1750–1850', *Archaeologia Cambrensis*, lxxx (1925), 121–48; D. Williams, *The Rebecca Riots* (1955), chap vi. Frequent comments on the value of road improvements are to be found in Sir John Sinclair's *Statistical Account of Scotland* (1791–99); see especially xix. 552.

41. *The Torrington Diaries*, ed. C. B. Andrews (1934–8), i. 17, ii. 170–1.

42. The earliest date given for it in the *Oxford English Dictionary* is 1800, but Byng was using the word in 1787: *Torrington Diaries*, i. 249.

43. *Ibid.*, iii. 50.

44. R. Fenton, *Historical Tour through Pembrokeshire* (1811), 4–7.

45. H. Robinson, *The British Post Office* (1948), 95–109.

46. T. S. Ashton, *An Economic History of England: the 18th Century* (1955), 71.

47. T. C. Barker, 'The Sankey Navigation', *Transactions of the Historic Society of Lancashire and Cheshire*, c (1948), 121–55.

48. C. Hadfield, *British Canals* (ed. 2, 1959), 175–6.

49. Jackman, *Transportation in Modern England*, 724–9.

50. *Journal of Transport History*, ii (1955–56), 166; A. T. Patterson, *Radical Leicester* (1954), 30–1.

51. Quoted in L. T. C. Rolt, *Inland Waterways of England* (ed. 2, 1955), 147.

52. See the diagram in A. Cossons, *Turnpike Roads of Nottinghamshire* (1934), 10.

53. P. Russell, *A Leicestershire Road* (1934), 88–90, 96, 115.

54. Quoted in G. C. Harper, *Stage-Coach and Mail in Days of Yore* (1903), i. 82–9.

55. Cf. R. H. Spiro, 'John Loudon McAdam and the Metropolis Turnpike Trust', *Journal of Transport History*, ii (1955–56), 207–13.

56. *Works* (1869 ed.), 793.

57. Cf. H. W. Hart, 'Some Notes on Coach Travel, 1750–1848', *Journal of Transport History*, iv (1959–60), 146–60.

58. Cf. S. Pollard and J. D. Marshall, 'The Furness Railway and the Growth of Barrow', *ibid.*, i (1953–54), 109–26.

59. This paragraph is based on the excellent account given in W. H. Chaloner, *Social and Economic Development of Crewe* (1950).

60. Statistics from *Bradshaw's Shareholder's Manual*, 1900.

61. Cf. G. C. Dickinson, 'Stage-Coach Services in the West Riding of Yorkshire between 1830 and 1840', *Journal of Transport History*, iv (1959–60), 1–12.

62. British Transport Commission Historical Relics Dept., Photographic Collection, AD 466/58.

63. Jackman, *Transportation in Modern England*, 617.

64. Russell, *A Leicestershire Road*, 144; *Notes and Queries for Somerset and Dorset*, xii. 317–9, xvii. 52.

65. Cf. Williams, *The Rebecca Riots*.

66. S. and B. Webb, *Story of the King's Highway* (1913), 222.

67. This story is well told in C. Hadfield, *Canals of South Wales and the Border* (1960), 108–17, and D. S. Barrie, *The Taff Vale Railway* (ed. 2, 1950).

68. The figures are given in Hadfield, *British Canals*, 215.

69. *Ibid.*, 210.

70. Robbins, *Middlesex*, 78.

71. *Ibid.*, 80.

72. P. Cunningham, *Hand-book of London* (ed. 2, 1850), xxxiv.

73. G. C. Dickinson, 'Development of Suburban Road Passenger Transport in Leeds, 1840–95', *Journal of Transport History*, iv (1959–60), 214–23.

74. The system is clearly described by D. L. G. Hunter: *ibid.*, ii (1953–54), 170–84.

75. W. T. Hughes, *A Century of Traction Engines* (1959), 93.

76. 3 *Hansard* clxiv. 288.

77. G. Maxcy and A. Silberston, *The Motor Industry* (1959), 225.

NOTES

78. The Secretary of the Board, Rhys Jeffreys, wrote a lively account of its work in *The King's Highway* (1949). Allowance must be made there for his vehement partisanship; the story deserves a fuller and more dispassionate examination when the necessary documents are available.

79. *Manchester Corporation Tramways: Report on the Comparative Utility of the Motor Bus and Tramcar* (1923), 2.

80. *Fifty Years of Municipal Transport* (Derby Corporation Omnibus Department, 1949), 14; *Crosville Handbook for 1955* (n.d.), 8, 132; C. I. Savage, *An Economic History of Transport* (1959), 113.

81. E. L. Cornwell, *Commercial Road Vehicles* (1960), 94–5.

82. C. D. Buchanan, *Mixed Blessing: the Motor in Britain* (1958), 210.

Index

The figures in italics refer to the illustrations on page 71 onwards